EMBROIDERY

EMBROIDERY

OVER FORTY EMBROIDERY PROJECTS FOR YOU AND YOUR HOME

INTRODUCTION BY UNA STUBBS

GALLERY BOOKS
An Imprint of W. H. Smith Publishers Inc.
112 Madison Avenue
New York City 10016

First published in 1989 by
Conran Octopus Limited
37 Shelton Street
London WC2H 9HN

This edition published by Gallery Books,
an imprint of W. H. Smith Publishers, Inc.
112 Madison Avenue, New York, New York 10016

ISBN 0-8317-2770-5

Typeset by SX Composing Limited
Printed in Hong Kong

CONTENTS

INTRODUCTION

At last! Here is an embroidery book which caters for all areas of the home and each member of the family, and I'm not talking about babies' bibs and tray cloths. This is a book with totally original ideas: some are exquisitely simple, and others more advanced, yet none is so unusual that in years to come you'll want to fling your effort to the back of the closet because it has become dated. I suppose, like any good design – be it for a car, a dress or a piece of furniture – if something has style it never dates. The French have always known that, and what we have here is a stunning collection of French designs.

From the age of 20 I have avidly bought French magazines: it didn't matter a jot that they were only printed in French (of which I speak not one word). I would gaze for hours at the photographs: not just of fashion, but of cooking, interiors and, of course, needlework. I gawped so longingly at Jeanne Moreau's or Brigitte Bardot's luscious houses that I now have a home pretending to be French Provençal in the center of London! And I copied French clothes by adapting English patterns: for the 60s film *Summer Holiday*, I auditioned wearing my homemade Chanel suit, and clutching an old black bag I had hung with a brassy chain handle.

Then one week there was an article about a lady called Felicia who had embroidered holiday scenes rather than use a camera, and there was a photograph of a wall in her kitchen smothered with enchanting embroidered 'holiday snaps' – it was a feast for the eyes. She has encouraged me in a hobby which is an indisputable joy, and so I must thank Madame Felicia for introducing me to French embroidery so many years ago.

Oh, that I had more hours in the day! I simply don't know which design to copy first from this wonderful collection, they are all so special. I love the Hungarian Duvet Cover and the Dragonfly Bedlinen. I am not as yet a grannie, but I could make the Baby Alphabet coverlet and store it away for later. And how I wish that when I lived in rented accommodation I had known how to cover to advantage the old furniture and ugly fireplaces with lovely embroidery as shown in this book.

I hope my eyesight holds out – I want to go stitching away until the grave! There is so much to choose from here. I can't ever remember looking through an embroidery book that so made me want to get cracking straight away. Many congratulations and thank you to EMBROIDERY for the hours of pleasure you will give to me.

Lynda Stubbs

8

BASIC ESSENTIALS

The techniques used in this book are all very straightforward, and the patterns easy to use. Most of the designs are shown smaller than actual size: the method used to enlarge them is explained below, as are the standard embroidery techniques and stitches required. Throughout, it is assumed that seams which are not enclosed will be edge-finished if the fabric tends to ravel, and that ordinary open seams, described below, will be used unless otherwise stated in the pattern. Skills specific to a particular project are described within the main text.

STARTING OFF

THREADS

Embroidery threads are available in a wide range of weights and colors. The most common threads are cotton or wool, but pure silk, linen, synthetic and metallic threads can also be bought. Some threads are twisted and cannot be divided; while others are made up of several strands which can be separated to give a finer thread. The strands can be put together to give different weight and color combinations, or thread mixes.

The following threads are used in this book:

Stranded cotton
A lustrous, six-stranded thread which can be separated.

Pearl cotton
A twisted, shiny thread which cannot be divided and is used as a single thread.

Danish flower thread
A soft, fine linen thread.

Tapestry wool
A twisted 4-ply pure wool thread which is hardwearing and mothproofed.

Rug wool
A twisted heavyweight pure wool yarn used for either stitched or tufted rugs.

FABRICS

There are three types of fabrics used for embroidery: plain-weave fabrics, even-weave fabrics and canvas. Plain-weave is the term used to describe any woven fabric, regardless of fibre content. The outline of an embroidery design is usually transferred on to this type of fabric, to act as a guide during the stitching.

Even-weave fabrics, although also plain-weave, have an important difference in the construction of the weave. The warp and weft threads are of identical thickness and the weave of the fabric is perfectly regular. The same number of warp and weft threads occur in a given area, making a regular grid so that stitches can be worked accurately by counting the threads and following a chart. The even-weave fabric group also contains fabrics, usually made of cotton or cotton blends, which have the threads woven together in pairs or in regular blocks.

Canvas is made from stiffened cotton warp and weft threads woven together to produce spaced holes between the threads, giving the fabric a regular grid-like structure. This grid is usually completely covered by the embroidery stitches, often worked from a chart. Canvas is available in different grid sizes (gauges), which indicate the number of threads which can be stitched in a 1in (2.5cm) square. Single canvas has a single-thread grid, and double canvas has pairs of threads forming the grid.

NEEDLES

Crewel, chenille and tapestry needles are the types of needles used for embroidery. They have larger eyes than ordinary sewing needles to accommodate a thicker thread.

Crewel needles
These are medium-length needles used for fine and medium-weight embroidery on plain-weave fabrics.

Chenille needles
Longer and thicker, and with larger eyes than crewel needles, chenille needles are suitable for use with heavier threads and fabrics.

Tapestry needles
Similar in shape to chenille needles, but with a blunt end rather than a sharp point. They are used for embroidery on even-weave fabrics and canvas.

All needles are graded from fine to coarse, with the lower number denoting the coarser needles. Needle sizes are suggested in this book, but you may actually prefer to use a different size according to your personal preference.

EMBROIDERY FRAMES

All embroidery will be more successful if the fabric or canvas is held taut in an embroidery frame. It is not only easier to handle, but the stitches will be more regular and distortion of the fabric is kept to a minimum. There are several types of frame available, and the choice depends on the fabric, the size of the project and your own preference. A simple round frame or hoop is suitable for embroidery on plain-weave fabrics. If the project is quite large, the hoop can be quickly and easily moved along the fabric after a portion of the stitching has been completed. Canvas should be stretched in a rectangular frame, large enough to accommodate the whole piece. The simplest rectangular frame is a wooden stretcher to which the canvas is attached by thumb tacks or staples. You can make a frame for yourself from four wooden stretchers joined at the corners. They are available in a wide range of sizes in art stores. Specialist embroidery frames (square or rotating frames) are adjustable and stretch the fabric very evenly. A hoop or a rectangular frame can be used with even-weave fabric, depending on the size of the project.

ENLARGING A DESIGN

Enlarging the designs in this book to the correct size is not difficult to do successfully, but accurate measuring is important. Basically, the technique consists of dividing the original design into equal squares and then carefully copying the design, square for square, onto a larger grid. First trace the design from the book on to a piece of tracing paper, centering it; then follow the diagrams shown on this page. The most accurate way to copy this image is to mark on the larger grid the equivalent points at which the design bisects a line on the smaller grid, and then to join up these marks.

Draw a grid square over the design you have traced, and then draw in a diagonal. Using this line as a guide, mark in the outline of the full-size square or rectangle on a larger piece of tracing paper, and then draw in a grid of the same number of squares, but larger in size, as on the small trace.

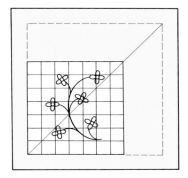

For example, if there is already a grid shown in the book and each square represents a square of 2in (5cm), then draw the large-scale grid to these dimensions. If the design has no grid, but is, say, half size, then draw a squared grid on tracing paper and tape it over the design. Trace the design, and then draw up a large grid, doubling the size and making sure that the top right corner meets a diagonal drawn from the smaller grid.

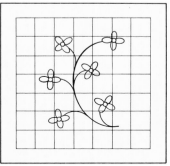

Copy the design square for square onto the larger grid. Once the entire pattern has been transferred, very carefully check it back against the original for accuracy.

TRANSFERRING A DESIGN

When the design has been enlarged to the desired size, you will need to transfer it onto the fabric before beginning the embroidery.

Four transfer methods are described here:

Carbon paper
Position the pattern paper centrally over the right side of the fabric to be embroidered, and pin it to the fabric at each corner. Carefully slide a sheet of dressmakers' carbon paper, carbon side down, between the pattern and the fabric. Draw over the design lines of the pattern with a tracing wheel or a knitting needle used as if it were a pencil.

Transfer pencil
Having drawn the pattern on heavy-duty tracing paper, turn the paper over and trace over the lines with a transfer pencil.

With this traced side facing down onto the fabric, position the pattern paper as required and pin down at each corner. Turn on an iron to a low heat, and press down on the transfer for a few seconds, then lift and move to the next area. Lift up the corner of the paper to make sure that the design is transferring.

Pricking and pouncing
This method is time-consuming but very accurate. Lay the pattern onto a thick wad of fabric – an old blanket would be ideal – and prick holes along the lines of the design using a sharp needle or stiletto. Keep the holes close together to obtain as accurate a copy as possible. Position the design onto the fabric right side up, and pin along the edges to fix the pattern securely. With a felt pad, gently rub pounce (a special-purpose powder available from

craft stores) over the pricked holes. Carefully remove the pattern so as not to smudge the pounce, then join up the dots with a dressmaker's pencil.

Using a light source
Although accurate, this method will only work with finely-woven fabric of a pale color. Attach the pattern to a light source such as a window or a light-box, and position the fabric on top. Use a dressmaker's pencil to trace the design.

EMBROIDERY STITCHES

The stitches used on the projects in this book are shown below. Although all are quite simple to work, some – such as satin stitch and long and short stitch – may need a little practice to work them neatly and get good fabric coverage. Follow the diagrams carefully if the stitch is one with which you are unfamiliar.

Work the fabric or canvas in an embroidery hoop or frame as this will help you to keep the stitches regular. Remember not to pull the threads too tightly, since this can distort the shape. The individual instructions will give you details of how to work the designs, where to start stitching, how many strands of thread to use, and suggested needle sizes.

Do not use a knot on the back of the fabric or canvas: it produces an unsightly bulge on the right side. Instead, leave a short tail of thread hanging, use the needleful of thread and then carefully secure both the ends on the wrong side by threading them through the stitches.

Before beginning a project, it is a good idea to practise sewing stitches with which you are unfamiliar on a spare piece of canvas or fabric. You may also wish to experiment with different colors and combinations of threads, and even with alternative stitches. In this way, you can either subtly or radically alter the pattern, creating designs to fit your particular taste and requirements.

straight stitch

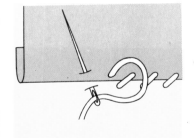

hemming stitch

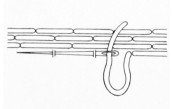

darning stitch

satin stitch

feather stitch

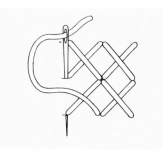

cross stitch

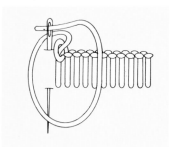

buttonhole stitch

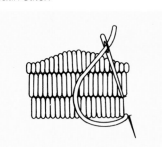

encroaching satin stitch

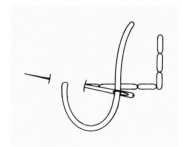

back stitch

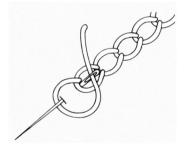

chain stitch

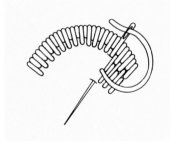

long and short stitch

padded satin stitch

Chinese knots

tent stitch

trammed half cross stitch

NOTE: Some of the stitches used in this book have been shown with specific projects: **antique hem stitch** (drawn-thread) see page 108, **closed herringbone stitch** see page 158, **French knots** see page 184.

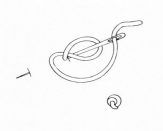

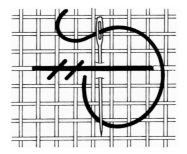

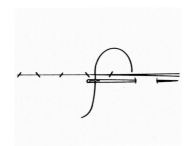

stem stitch

couching

slip stitch

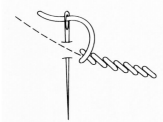

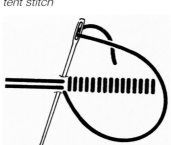

half cross stitch

seed stitch

herringbone stitch

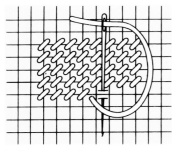

FINISHING OFF

PRESSING

Embroidery on fabric will need a light pressing to smooth out any wrinkles in the fabric caused by the stitching.

Before pressing, pad the ironing board with a thick, folded towel and lay the embroidery over it face down.

Cover the embroidery with a damp piece of thin cotton fabric and press lightly, letting the iron just touch the pressing cloth. Take care not to crush heavily stitched areas. Let the embroidery dry thoroughly.

SEAMS

Plain seam

Place the two fabric pieces with right sides together, raw edges even; pin and stitch together ⅝in (1.5cm) from the raw edges. Work a few stitches in reverse at each end of the seam to secure the threads.

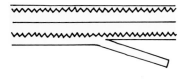

The simplest method of neatening the seam allowance edges is by zigzag stitching on a sewing-machine. Use a short, narrow stitch worked slightly in from the raw edge. If the fabric has a tendency to fray, use a larger stitch and work over the raw edge. Where the fabric is fine, turn under the raw edge and either zigzag stitch or straight stitch. If finishing by hand, overcast the raw edges: work from left to right, taking the thread diagonally over the edge and keeping the stitches about ⅛in (3mm) apart. If the fabric tends to fray, work a row of straight stitching first, then oversew over the edge. If the fabric is very heavy, simply pink the edges using a pair of pinking shears.

Flat fell seam

This is a self-neatening seam that is very strong and distinctive. Place the two fabric pieces with right sides together ⅝in (1.5cm) from the raw edges. Press the seam allowance to one side. Trim down the lower seam allowance to ¼in (6mm). Fold the upper seam allowance over, enclosing the lower seam allowance. Press the folded allowance flat against the fabric; pin and stitch close to the folded edge.

French seam

This is a self-finishing seam. Place the two fabric pieces with wrong sides together; pin and stitch ¼in (6mm) from the raw edges. Press the seam open. Refold with right sides together; pin and stitch ⅜in (1cm) from the seamed edge.

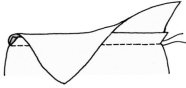

FASTENINGS

How to insert a zipper

Pin and tack the seam into which the zipper is to be inserted. Stitch in from each, or from one, end of the seam,

leaving an opening the same length as the zipper. Press seam open. Place the zipper face down over the seam allowances with the bottom stop ⅛in (3mm) beyond the tacking at one side and with the teeth centered over the tacked seam. Tack in place through all layers ¼in (6mm) on either side of the teeth. Turn to the right side. Stitch the zipper in place using a zipper foot on the sewing-machine or back-stitch by hand, following the tacking lines at the sides and pivoting the stitching at the bottom corners or at both ends.

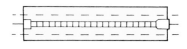

BIAS STRIPS

To cut the fabric on the bias, fold the fabric so that the selvage (warp threads) lies exactly parallel to the weft threads. The fold formed is the true cross. Cut along the fold and then cut the bias strips parallel to this edge.

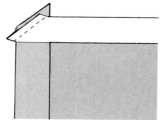

Mark off the strips using pins or a marking pen and cut out. To join strips together, place two strips with right sides together on the straight of grain, as shown, and stitch together taking ¼in (6mm) seams. Trim off points level with side edges and press seam open.

MITERING THE CORNERS

This method of finishing corners will ensure a neat, crisp finish.

Mitering fabric

Fold over a narrow hem along each edge of the fabric and

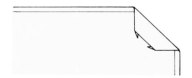

press. Trim the corner to reduce bulk, then turn the corner over and press. Fold over the two sides as shown, and pin in place. Hand or machine stitch along the hem. Hand stitch the diagonal joining if the hem is quite wide.

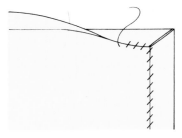

Mitering canvas

Always block the canvas (see below) before finishing the edges. Trim the corner of the surplus canvas to reduce the bulk. Turn the canvas over to the corner of the embroidery.

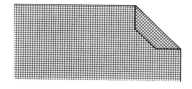

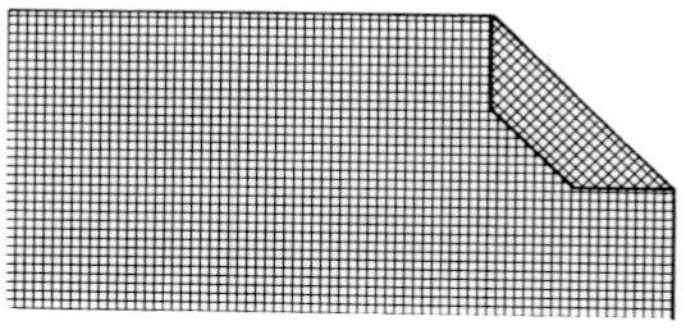

Fold in the side edges, making sure that the corner is square, and tack in place. Then secure the edge and the mitered corner with a row of hand stitching.

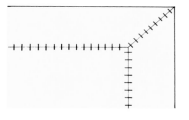

Mitering a fabric band

Fold the fabric band in half lengthwise, raw edges together. Fold up the raw edges in line with the folded edge and press. Cut along the fold lines. Repeat at the opposite end of the strip, but so that the diagonal edge is facing in the opposite direction. Repeat with all strips. Unfold two adjoining strips and place with right sides together and pointed ends matching. Pin and stitch the end, beginning and ending the stitching ⅝in (1.5cm)

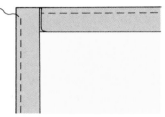

from either end of the seam. Trim and turn to right side, refolding the strip in half. Repeat, to form each mitered corner. Place one edge to the main piece of fabric with right sides together; pin and stitch. Turn under remaining edge of band and slipstitch over previous stitches on the wrong side.

Mitering binding

Unfold one edge of binding and place against the raw fabric edge. Pin and stitch in place along the first side up to the seam allowance at the turning point. Press up the binding over the stitched side at a 45 degree angle. Stitch the next side beginning at the turning point. Trim and turn the binding over the raw edge to the wrong side folding the excess binding on both sides into miters. Slipstitch

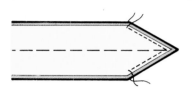

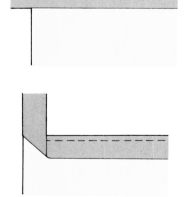

the remaining folded edge of binding over previous stitches on the wrong side. If the binding is wide, stitch across the corner on the right side of the fabric before turning the binding over the raw edge. Trim and press open. Pleat the excess fabric into a miter on the wrong side.

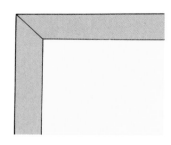

BLOCKING

Canvaswork should be blocked to straighten the grain of the canvas, which becomes distorted during the stitching, even when an embroidery frame has been used. For blocking, you will need: a piece of wood or blockboard larger than the embroidery and covered with a sheet of clean polythene; rustproof tacks; a hammer; a steel rule or tape measure; a water spray or sponge.

If the canvas has a selvage, cut small nicks along it to ensure that it stretches evenly. Damp the canvaswork with the spray or a wet sponge and

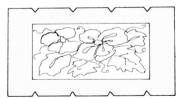

place it face down on the board. Lightly hammer tacks in the middle of the top and bottom of the surplus canvas, stretching the canvas gently downwards. Repeat for each side, checking that the warp and weft threads of the canvas are at right angles to each other.

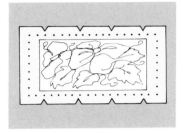

Working outwards from the center of each side, insert more tacks at ¾in (2cm) intervals, stretching the canvas gently as you proceed. When you have done all four sides, check the size and shape of the canvas to make sure the stretching is even and adjust the tacks where necessary. Hammer all the tacks in securely. Spray or sponge the canvas so that it is evenly damp, and leave it to dry at room temperature for several days. A second blocking may be needed to straighten strongly vertical or horizontal designs.

CUSHION COVER

This cushion cover is made quite simply from one folded piece of fabric, and does not require a zipper or fasteners. For a snug fit, the cushion pad should measure about 1in (2.5cm) more in each direction

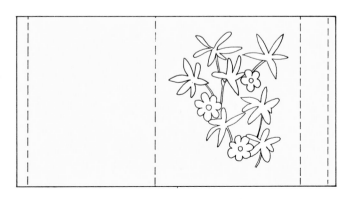

than one side of the sewn cover.

Finish the short edges of the fabric by turning a narrow hem and machine stitching.

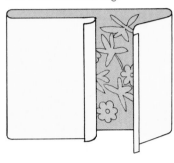

Fold the fabric as shown, with the right side facing in, making sure that the wider flap will be

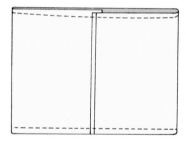

on top when you turn the cover right side out. Pin the sides.

Machine stitch along either side of the cushion cover, stitching across the overlapping fabric folds which will form a flap.

Turn the cushion cover right side out, gently pushing the corners out fully. Press well.

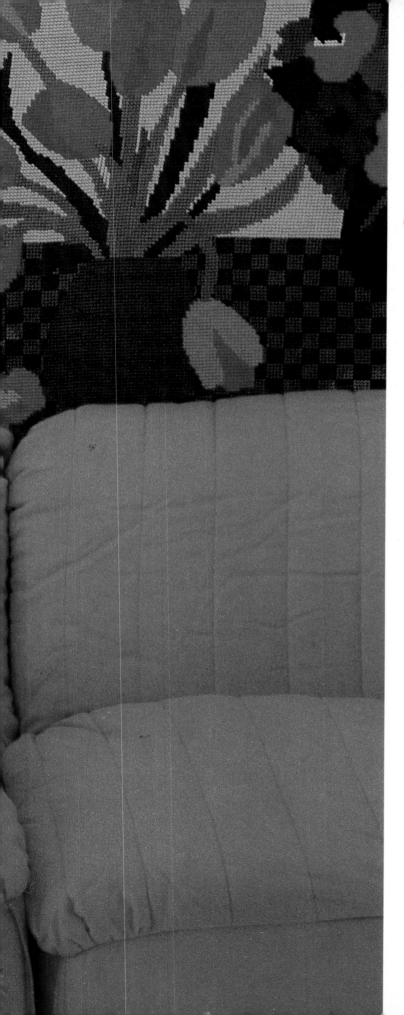

CANVASWORK

CRAZY CROSS STITCH

A far cry from the conventional flower-patterned needlepoint, this unusual cross-stitch design features a bold, humorous medley of letters, symbols and colors, with elements of both 1930s and 1950s decorative styles. The result is a colorful rug that will harmonize with most modern settings. If you want to add a personal touch, you could easily substitute your initials for some of the letters, keeping to the same large block capitals with drawing pin circles at the joins.

Size Approximately 63½in × 55in (159cm × 138cm).

MATERIALS

2yd × 1¾yd (1.8m × 1.6m) of 4-gauge rug canvas Strong sewing thread	Large tapestry or rug needle Fine-tip waterproof felt marker Wide masking tape

Threads
*Pingouin rug yarn (if this is not available, substitute the same colors from another range): 16 balls of **gray** 30; nine balls of **black** 36; four balls each of **red** 43, **yellow** 61 and **orange** 52; three balls each of **bright*** *blue* 60, **pink** 51 and **white** 05; two balls each of **turquoise** 55, **sky blue** 65, **jade green** 71, **green** 58 and **rose pink** 15; one ball each of **brown** 08, **French blue** 34 and **brick** 14*

Embroidery stitches
Cross stitch worked in two journeys (see below); each square on the chart represents one cross stitch.
Herringbone stitch for finishing the edges.

DIRECTIONS

▦ Draw a vertical line with the waterproof marker down the center of the canvas, taking care not to cross any vertical threads. Mark the central horizontal line in the same way. Rule corresponding lines across the chart to find the center of the design.

▦ Bind the edges of the canvas with masking tape to prevent the threads unravelling. Begin stitching at the center of the canvas, working outwards from the center of the design and following the chart square by square. To make the canvas easier to handle, roll up those areas on which you are not working.

▦ Make each horizontal line of cross stitch in two journeys. Stitch the left to right diagonals on the first journey and complete the crosses on the second journey by filling in the right to left diagonals.

▦ When all the stitching has been completed, block the embroidery (see page 15) if it has pulled out of shape. Trim the surplus canvas away leaving a margin of 4in (10cm) of unworked canvas all around the embroidery.

▦ On the reverse of the rug, turn in the margin (see page 14 for instructions on mitering corners) and secure the edges with a row of herringbone stitch in strong thread.

▦ Alternatively, use strips of carpet webbing, overlapping them at the corners. Backstitch the strips to the rug, then miter and stitch them as shown.

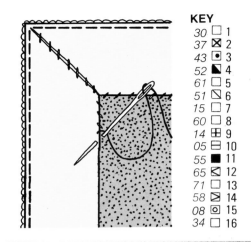

KEY

30	☐	1
37	☒	2
43	⊡	3
52	◣	4
61	☐	5
51	◿	6
15	☐	7
60	☐	8
14	⊞	9
05	⊟	10
55	■	11
65	◸	12
71	☐	13
58	◨	14
08	⊙	15
34	☐	16

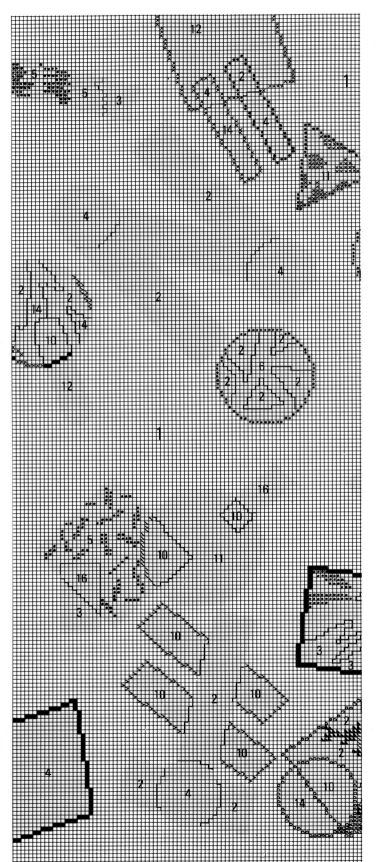

COUNTRYSIDE MOSAIC

Each of the nine canvas squares that make up this tapestry mosaic contain a different wildlife scene, but they cleverly combine to create a complete picture – poppies and ladybirds, frogs on lily pads, butterflies and milkweed, snails and dandelions are just some of them. If you feel that the complete mosaic is beyond you, make up just a couple of the individual scenes.

MATERIALS

9 squares of single thread 12-gauge canvas, each 14½in (36cm) × 14½in (36cm)
Tapestry needle size 18 or 20
3ft (90cm) × 3ft (90cm) beige

cotton fabric
Matching sewing thread
Fine-tip waterproof felt marker
Embroidery frame

Threads
DMC tapestry wool in the colors given beside each panel.

Embroidery Stitches
Tent stitch, Chinese knots, straight stitch, herringbone stitch, back stitch.

Each square of the design is complete in itself, but can be combined with others to make a larger scene. When all the squares are embroidered and blocked, arrange them as shown in the diagrams opposite. Join the squares with flat seams using backstitch (see page 12), and press open.

For a larger bedspread, slipstitch the completed embroidery onto a plain bedspread. Move the panel around the bedspread until the desired effect is achieved. For a wall hanging, make a casing at the top and bottom edges and insert two bamboo canes and hang with a cord.

DIRECTIONS

▧ Draw a vertical line with the marker through the center of each canvas square, taking care not to cross any vertical threads. Mark the central horizontal line in the same way. Then rule corresponding lines across the chart to find the center of the design.

▧ Work each of the individual canvas squares in an embroidery frame.

▧ Work the designs outwards from the center in tent stitch and pick out the details in Chinese knots and straight stitch as indicated on the charts.

▧ When all the squares have been embroidered, block each one carefully (see page 15), making sure that they are all the same size: each blocked square should measure approximately 10in (25cm) × 10in (25cm).

▧ Following the diagram, join the squares into three strips of three squares, by making a back-stitched seam between each square. Press each seam open.

▧ Join the strips together in the same way, and again press each seam open.

▧ On the reverse of the cover, turn in the surplus canvas round the edge (see page 14 for instructions on mitering corners) and secure it with a row of herringbone stitch.

▧ To make the lining, cut a 33in (82cm) square from the beige fabric. Turn and press a hem round the edge to make a 31in (78cm) square. Slipstitch the lining to the bedcover and press it gently, taking care not to crush the stitches.

1

1. Dandelions and snail
green 7320, 7347, 7370, 7548;
brown 7419, 7468, 7526;
turquoise 7302; *orange* 7767;
beige 7465; *cream* 7141; *blue*

7800; *gray* 7331, 7620; *yellow*
7473, 7727, 7742, 7905; *white*

2. Bee with flowers
cream 7503; *pink* 7135, 7136,

7640; *gray* 7618, 7624; *blue*
7799; *green* 7339, 7363, 7396,
7398; *turquoise* 7592; *brown*
7417, 7419, 7479, 7485, 7713,
7999; *black*; *white*

3. Ladybird and poppies
green 7347, 7427, 7770; *tan*
7947; *red* 7107, 7606; *blue*
7799; *brown* 7401, 7415, 7419,
7801; *gray* 7618, 7713; *yellow*

7078, 7485; **white**; **black**; **ecru**

4. Dragonfly and flowers
yellow 7484, 7504, 7579, 7678, 7843; **brown** 7417, 7469, 7479,

7526; **green** 7353, 7362, 7363, 7389, 7404, 7408, 7427, 7429; **blue** 7243, 7791; **turquoise** 7302, 7326, 7329, 7592, 7690; **mauve** 7245; **cream** 7493;

kingfisher 7650; **black**; **white**

5. Grasshopper and berries
brown 7513, 7526, 7548, 7713, 7833, 7999; **green** 7346, 7353,

7362, 7363, 7376, 7384, 7392, 7396, 7493, 7861; **yellow** 7473, 7485, 7785; **beige** 7450; **red** 7606, 7666, 7946; **turquoise** 7302, 7592; **black**; **white**

6

7

8

9

6. Frog and waterlily
brown *7249, 7355, 7490, 7801;*
green *7362, 7636, 7384, 7540;*
yellow *7485, 7677, 7678;* **pink**
7356, 7543, 7950; **black; white**

7. Newt and flowers
green *7320, 7362, 7363, 7384,*

7389, 7393, 7398, 7890; **brown**
7249, 7512, 7526, 7999; **yellow**
7678, 7782, 7784, 7785; **cream**
7501; **beige** *7450;* **turquoise**
7592; **black; white**

8. Butterflies and flowers
brown *7514, 7538, 7713, 7780;*

green *7320, 7363, 7384, 7387,*
7583, 7890; **yellow** *7504, 7678,*
7786; **pink** *7255;* **mauve** *7245;*
turquoise *7996;* **orange** *7505,*
7946; **red** *7666;* **blue** *7317,*
7796; **tan** *7457;* **black; white;**
ecru

9. Beetles and flowers
yellow *7677, 7784, 7786;* **green**
7320, 7367, 7386, 7389, 7424,
7548, 7583, 7890, 7956; **brown**
7479, 7526, 7713, 7845, 7846;
beige *7450, 7463;* **mauve** *7245;*
pink *7255;* **blue** *7317, 7820,*
7995; **white; ecru**

FRESH FLOWERS

Transform an old chair by stitching a new needle-point cover, decorated with a colorful bouquet of flowers, and turn an eyesore into an elegant conversation piece: the idea is scarcely new, but the reason for its perennial success is that it works so well and so beautifully. The background in this case is given interest by a simple geometric design and in order to vary the effect the French artist used a larger scale of canvas for the seat than for the back and sides of the chair, changing the size of the pattern.

Size Adjustable to fit any chair; the flower bouquet measures approximately 10in (25cm) from top to bottom and 8in (20cm) across.

MATERIALS

Single-thread 16-gauge canvas for the back and side panels
Single-thread 14-gauge canvas for the seat cushion
Tapestry needles size 20 and 18
Rotating embroidery frame or

wooden stretchers large enough to accommodate each piece of canvas
Fine-tip waterproof felt marker
Medium-tip felt marker

Note Chairs differ greatly in shape and design, and unless you have advanced upholstery skills you will probably choose to have your chair reupholstered professionally, so we have not explained how to fit the cover. Take all measurements very carefully (if possible, remove the old upholstery and measure this flat), making generous allowance for tuck-ins and seam allowances.

Threads

For the bouquet, *DMC tapestry wools: one skein each of* **red** *7107, 7606 and 7946*, **orange** *7439*, **mauve** *7120*, **violet** *7243, 7251, 7255 and 7709*, **peach** *7917*, **pink** *7133, 7204, 7260, 7600, 7603 and 7804*, **blue** *7304, 7313, 7314, 7317 and 7800*, **green** *7327, 7369, 7384, 7386 7420, 7424, 7549, 7583, 7771, 7912 and 7956*, **yellow** *7433, 7681 and 7725*, **beige** *7423 and 7579*, **cream** *7745*, **ecru** *and* **white**

For the back, side panels, cushion cover and bouquet background the following colors of DMC tapestry wool are used: **green** *7369, 7386, 7420 and 7424.*

Embroidery Stitches

Half cross stitch, slanting satin stitch and straight stitch.

Note
To calculate the amount of thread needed for your chair, embroider a 4in (10cm) square of the pattern to use as a guide, stitching as follows: main color 7424, second color 7369, third color 7386 and fourth color 7420.

DIRECTIONS

▦ Measure each section of the chair widthwise and lengthwise. Draw the outline of each section on the appropriate canvas, bearing in mind that the finished pieces of embroidery should be approximately ⅜in (1cm) larger than these measurements to allow for turnings. Allow at least 4in (10cm) of surplus canvas around each piece for mounting in the embroidery frame, for blocking, and for the upholstery.
▦ Trace the bouquet design for the back of the chair and enlarge it to the required dimensions (see page 10). Strengthen the design lines with the medium felt marker.
▦ Place the canvas for the back panel over the design, centering the bouquet inside the drawn outline. The design lines will now be visible through the canvas.

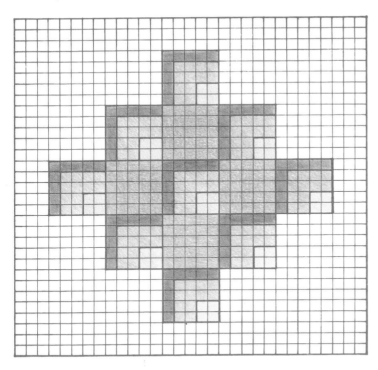

Using the waterproof felt marker, trace the design carefully onto the canvas.

▦ Mount the canvas in the embroidery frame or stretcher and begin the embroidery by working the flowers in irregular straight stitch. Work with the tapestry wool divided in half in the smaller needle and use the photograph as a color blending and stitch guide. When all the flowers have been completed, fill in the background between them in half cross stitch, using the green thread 7424.

▦ Work the geometric pattern around the central motif in slanting satin stitch and half cross stitch. Follow the chart carefully and again work with the tapestry wool divided in half.

▦ Work the geometric pattern on the two side panels in the same way.

▦ Embroider the geometric pattern for the cushion sections on the coarser canvas, using the tapestry wool undivided in the larger needle.

▦ When all the embroidery has been completed block the sections (see page 15) if they have pulled out of shape, paying special attention to the geometric pattern, which should be perfectly regular.

KEY

1	*7107*
2	*7439*
3	*7606*
4	*7946*
5	*7600*
6	*7603*
7	*7804*
8	*7133*
9	*7204*
10	*7260*
11	*7255*
12	*7709*
13	*7251*
14	*7120*
15	*7243*
16	*7917*
17	*7433*
18	*7725*
19	*7681*
20	*7745*
21	*7579*
22	*7423*
23	*ecru*
24	*white*
25	*7369*
26	*7384*
27	*7386*
28	*7420*
29	*7424*
30	*7549*
31	*7583*
32	*7771*
33	*7327*
34	*7912*
35	*7956*
36	*7304*
37	*7313*
38	*7314*
39	*7317*
40	*7800*

Enlarge 1½ times

FRUIT NEEDLEPOINT

The soft colors of this needlepoint fruit basket suggest the aging tones of gentle Dutch seventeenth-century still lifes. The embroidery is worked in half cross stitch on linen – the natural color of the fabric provides the perfect neutral background for the fine needlework.

MATERIALS

24cm (60cm) × 32in (80cm) light brown even-weave 24-gauge linen

Crewel needle size 5 or 6
Embroidery hoop

Threads
Danish flower threads –
1 skein of each of the following colors: **green** 40, 222, 223, 302; **red** 53, 93; **violet** 5, 230; **yellow** 28, 225; **fawn** 7
DMC stranded cotton –
3 skeins of **green** 989
2 skeins of each of the following colors:
green 472, 3346, 3348; **coral** 353; **peach** 754; **beige** 644
1 skein of each of the following colors:
green 368, 471, 581, 3051, 3052, 3053, 3347; **bronze** 733, 734; **rust** 355, 356; **tan** 922; **coral** 352; **peach** 758, 945, 950, 951; **pink** 316, 760, 778, 948; **mauve** 3041, 3042; **yellow** 745, 3078; **cream** 746; **gold** 437, 677, 833, 834, 3046; **fawn** 422, 738; **brown** 420, 640, 642; **beige** 437, 712, 739; **gray** 452, 453, 646, 647, 3023

Embroidery Stitch
Half cross stitch: each square on the chart represents one half cross stitch worked over two vertical and two horizontal fabric threads.

DIRECTIONS

 Run a vertical and a horizontal line of basting through the center of the linen to correspond with the center lines on the chart.

 Work with the fabric stretched in an embroidery hoop, moving the hoop as necessary.

 Embroider the design outwards from the center in half cross stitch, following the picture on page 33 and using the colors and threads indicated: the main part of the picture is worked using five strands of the stranded cotton, while some areas are stitched with a combination of Danish flower thread and stranded cotton threaded

through the needle together.

 When the embroidery is completed, place it face down on a well-padded surface and press lightly, taking care not to crush the stitches.

 If the fabric has become distorted during the stitching, it will need to be blocked (see page 15). The embroidery should be framed professionally.

A. Vine leaves, tendrils and stalks
green *40, 47, 223, 368, 471, 472, 581, 989, 3051, 3052, 3053, 3446, 3347, 3348*
brown *420, 640*
gray *646, 647*
fawn *422*

B. Basket
gray *646, 3023*
rust *356*
beige *644*
fawn *7*
green *222, 302, 3052*

C. Cherries
pink *948*
peach *754, 758*
rust *355, 356*
coral *352*
tan *922*
red *53, 93*
green *368*

D. Green grapes
bronze *734*
green *472*
cream *746*
fawn *422, 738*
gold *833, 834, 3046, 3047*
yellow *225, 3078*

E. Black grapes
mauve *3041, 3042*
violet *5, 230*
pink *316, 778*
green *581*

F. Apple
pink *760, 948*
peach *754, 950*
green *472*
coral *353*
beige *350, 712*
yellow *745, 3078*

G. Left pear
peach *945, 950, 951*
beige *437, 739*
gold *677*
green *223, 368, 3348*
yellow *28*
pink *948*
fawn *422*

H. Right pear
peach *945, 950*
beige *437, 712*
gold *677*
green *472*
yellow *3078*
fawn *422*
brown *642*
gray *452, 647*

I. Peach at the back
peach *754*
pink *760, 948*
coral *353*
yellow *745*
beige *712*
fawn *738*
gray *452, 453*

J. Front peach
peach *754, 950*
pink *760*
coral *352, 353*
yellow *745, 3078*
beige *712*
gray *452, 453, 647*

K. Fruit inside basket
green *472, 989, 3051, 3346, 3347*
rust *355*

The diagram indicates the different fruits and can be used with this list of colors.

TULIP TIME

Use it as a wall hanging, an unusual table runner or even as a mat: whichever you choose, this bright needlepoint picture with its vivid, life-size tulips and anemones will catch the eye and lift the spirits. The zingy reds and pinks, glowing all the more against the green contrast of the leaves, blend happily with the clean, simple lines of modern furnishings.

Size Approximately 80in × 24in (200cm × 60cm).

MATERIALS

2½yd × 28in (2.2m × 70cm) of double-thread 12-gauge canvas

2½yd (2.2m) of 36in (90cm) wide cotton fabric in a neutral color, for the lining

Matching strong sewing thread

Tapestry needle size 18 or 20

Fine-tip waterproof felt marker

Medium-tip black felt marker

Rotating embroidery frame, large enough to accommodate the width of the canvas

Wide masking tape

82in (205cm) strip of 4in (10cm) wide webbing, optional, for a casing if the panel is to be hung

Threads

DMC tapestry yarn: one skein each of **green** 7342, 7370, 7604 and 7912, **pink** 7153, **yellow** 7784 and 7973, and **mauve** 7247; two skeins each of **blue** 7797, **green** 7345, 7386 and 7540, **ecru, pink** 7103, 7106, 7135 and 7151, **red** 7137, **yellow** 7726, and **mauve** 7245; three skeins each of **green** 7596 and 7988, **pink** 7136, and **mauve** 7243; four skeins of **green** 7344; five skeins each of **red** 7640; six skeins each of **black**, and **green** 7861; seven skeins each of **red** 7606 and 7666; eight skeins of **pink** 7157; nine skeins each of **green** 7943 and 7547, and **pink** 7155; 17 skeins each of **blue** 7820 and 7995, and 29 skeins of **beige** 7280

Embroidery Stitches

Trammed half cross stitch for the plain background, flowers and pots; half cross stitch for the checkerboard background, and herringbone stitch for finishing the edges.

DIRECTIONS

THE EMBROIDERY

▦ Trace the design and then enlarge it to the dimensions given. Strengthen the design lines with the felt marker.

▦ Place the canvas over the design, leaving a 4in (10cm) margin of surplus canvas around all the edges. The design lines will now be visible through the canvas. Using the waterproof felt marker, trace the design carefully onto the canvas.

▦ Bind the two long edges of canvas with masking tape to prevent them fraying and then mount the canvas in the rotating embroidery frame.

▦ Starting at one edge and working each area of color separately, embroider the checkerboard background in half cross stitch and the rest of the design in trammed half cross stitch.

▦ When all the embroidery has been completed, remove the embroidery frame.

▦ Block the embroidery (see page 15) if it has pulled out of shape, paying special attention to the checkerboard pattern, in which the squares should be regular.

FINISHING THE PANEL

▦ Leaving a margin of 2in (5cm) all around the embroidered area, trim away the surplus canvas.

2

■ Mitering the corners, turn the unworked edges to the back and secure them with herringbone stitch.

■ To make the lining, cut a rectangle of lining fabric 1 in (2.5cm) larger than the finished embroidery on all edges. Turn in and press a generous 1 in (2.5cm) single hem all around, making sure that the finished size of the lining is slightly smaller than the embroidery.

■ If you wish to hang the picture, turn in the short ends of the webbing by 1 in (2.5cm). Position the webbing ¾in (2cm) below top edge of lining and machine stitch along the top edge. Lay the lining on a flat surface; take the hanging pole and fold the webbing over it. Pin along the bottom edge of the webbing; remove the pole, and then stitch along the pinned edge.

■ Fold the lining vertically in half, bringing right sides together. Using locking stitch, in which the thread is taken alternately through the back of the embroidery and then through the lining, join the lining to the back of the finished embroidery down the center. Working first out to one side then out to the other, join the lining to the back of the embroidery with additional vertical lines of stitching approximately 10in (25cm) apart, always taking care not to stitch through the webbing sleeve. Finish by slipstitching around all edges.

KEY

a 7342	**j** 7345	**t** 7245	**D** 7606
b 7370	**k** 7386	**u** 7596	**E** 7666
c 7604	**l** 7540	**v** 7988	**F** 7157
d 7912	**m** ecru	**w** 7136	**G** 7943
e 7153	**n** 7103	**x** 7243	**H** 7155
f 7784	**o** 7106	**y** 7344	**I** 7820
g 7973	**p** 7135	**z** 7547	**J** 7995
h 7247	**q** 7151	**A** 7640	
i 7797	**r** 7137	**B** black	
	s 7726	**C** 7861	

PANSY BAG

Pansies – *pensées* means thoughts – are just the motif for a useful carry-all for books, holiday things, or weekend bits and pieces. The bag is stitched in sturdy cotton first and the embroidered canvas panel is attached afterwards.

MATERIALS

32in (80cm) × 45in (115cm) heavy gray cotton fabric
7½in (19cm) × 18½in (46cm) gray lining fabric
20in (50cm) × 22in (55cm) double-thread 10-gauge canvas

6½in (16cm) × 17in (43cm) stout card
Gray sewing thread
Fine-tip waterproof pen
Fabric glue
Tapestry needle size 18 or 20
Embroidery frame

Threads
Susan Bates Anchor tapestry wool
TARTAN BACKGROUND
4 skeins of **gray** *400; 3 skeins of* **beige** *438; 5 skeins of* **blue** *147; 5 skeins of* **green** *164; 2 skeins of* **green** *506.*
THE PANSIES
1 skein of each color:
green *213, 215, 243, 265, 861;* **yellow** *264, 288, 290, 297, 305, 306, 729;* **beige** *377, 390, 711, 732;* **white** *402;* **pink** *337, 421, 570, 661, 732, 835, 892;* **blue** *850, 851*

Embroidery Stitch
Half cross stitch: each square on the chart represents one half cross stitch.

DIRECTIONS

THE PANSY EMBROIDERY:

▦ Draw a 17in (43cm) × 14½in (36cm) rectangle centered on the canvas with the felt marker. Then draw a vertical and a horizontal line in the center of this rectangle, taking care not to cross any threads running the opposite way. Rule corresponding lines across the printed chart to find the center.

▦ Work with the canvas in a frame. Begin stitching at the center of the canvas, working outwards and following the chart square by square. Embroider the pansy design first and then fill in the background with the tartan pattern.

▦ Block the finished piece of embroidery (see page 15).

▦ Trim the surplus canvas away leaving a margin of 1in (2.5cm) all round the embroidery. Turn in the margin (see page 14 for instructions on mitering corners) and tack round the edge.

TO MAKE THE BAG:

▦ Cut out the fabric as shown in the cutting layout. Join the front and back pieces together along the shortest sides using a fell seam with a seam allowance of ⅝in (1.5cm). Turn over ⅜in (1cm) followed by 1in (2.5cm) along the top of the bag, right-side up, to make a double hem; topstitch ¼in (5mm) away from the edge.

▦ Fold each strap piece in half lengthwise with the right side of the fabric on the inside. Stitch ⅜in (1cm) from the edge. Turn the straps to the right side and press flat. Top stitch all the way round ¼in (5mm) from the edge.

▦ Pin one strap to the front of the bag and one to the back along the lines indicated on the pattern and stitch in place securely.

▦ Turn the bag inside out and pin the base piece in place (with a seam allowance of ⅝in (1.5cm)). Stitch round the base twice. Turn the bag right side out and slipstitch the embroidered panel to the front.

▦ Cover the card with the lining fabric, as shown in the diagram, and let the glue dry thoroughly, then drop the base into the bag and push well down.

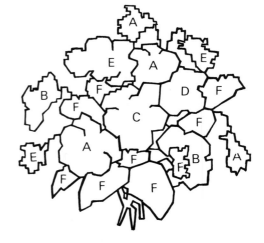

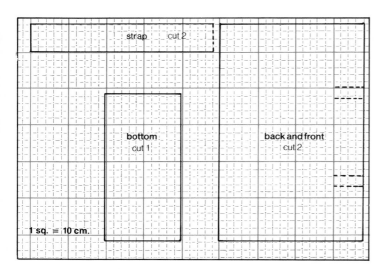

strap — cut 2

bottom — cut 1

back and front — cut 2

1 sq. = 10 cm.

Assemble the bag by joining the front and back sections. Make the straps and attach them securely before sewing the base in position. Slipstitch the canvas work panel to the front of the bag before inserting the stiffened base panel

Tartan pattern		Flowers C		Flowers D	
1	400	1	851	1	850
2	506	2	290	2	306
3	438	3	402	3	305
4	147	4	390	4	297
3	306	5	835	5	402
4	711	6	729	6	732
5	390	7	337	7	570
6	243	8	570		
7	297	9	243	**Flowers E**	
8	402			1	850
9	305			2	306
10	265			3	661
11	288			4	402

Leaves F		Flowers A		Flowers B	
1	213	1	850	1	661
2	215	2	264	2	570
3	861			3	421
4	438			4	305
5	377				

Flowers E (cont.): 5 732, 6 421, 7 892, 8 570, 9 711, 10 297, 11 243

COUNTRY CONTENTMENT

Sit down to a refreshing cup of tea, secure in the knowledge that there is another cup in the pot, kept warm by a teacosy like a romantic rural idyll: a thatched cottage complete with leaded windows and rambling roses. The scale of this cottage would suit a small teapot. For a family-sized one you could add sky and clouds, finishing with blue cord instead of pink around the edge. The finished cover, with its warm interlining, is guaranteed to keep your tea hot while you daydream about a lazy summer in the country.

Size Approximately 7in × 11in (18cm × 28cm), to suit a small teapot.

MATERIALS

13in × 18in (33cm × 46cm) of double-thread 9-gauge canvas
Tapestry needle size 22
Fine-point waterproof felt marker
Rectangular embroidery frame or stretcher
1½yd (1.3m) of ¼in (6mm)

diameter pink cording (made or purchased, see page 44)
¼yd (30cm) of 36in (90cm) wide pink lining fabric
Beige and pink sewing threads
¼yd (30c,) of 36in (90cm) wide medium-weight polyester or cotton wadding

Threads

Anchor stranded cotton: two skeins each of **pink** 35 and 54, **beige** 372 and 376, **green** 842, 887 and 888, **brown** 357, 379 and 380, **gray** 393, **brick** 339,

yellow 302 and 311, **mauve** 104, **black** 403, and **white** 1, and four skeins each of **brown** 368, and **beige** 387

Embroidery Stitches

Cross stitch and lattice stitch for the canvaswork and back stitch and herringbone for making up the cosy.

DIRECTIONS

▦ Using the felt marker, draw a line across the width of the canvas to divide it into two equal rectangles, one for the front of the teacosy and one for the back. Draw a vertical line through the center of each canvas rectangle, taking care not to cross any vertical threads. Mark the central horizontal line across each rectangle. Rule corresponding lines across the chart to find the center of the design.

▦ Mount the entire canvas in the embroidery frame or stretcher. On one canvas rectangle, embroider the cottage, starting at the center of the design and working outwards in cross stitch, following the chart square by square. Use

six strands of thread throughout. Work over the windows in lattice (large herringbone) stitch using the black thread.

▦ Embroider the cottage design again on the remaining canvas rectangle. When all the stitching is completed, block the canvas carefully, following the instructions given on page 15.

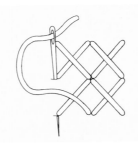

FINISHING

▢ Separate the two embroidered sections and trim away the unworked canvas from both pieces of embroidery, leaving a margin of ¾in (2cm) all around.

▢ Cut two pieces of lining to the same size and shape as the canvas (omitting the chimney tops), and two pieces of wadding ¾in (2cm) smaller all around.

▢ Place the two pieces of embroidery with right sides facing and, using beige thread, backstitch them neatly together, leaving the lower edge open. Turn under the lower edge right up to the embroidery and secure it with a row of herringbone stitch.

▢ Place one piece of wadding over one side of the embroidery, trimming it to the correct shape if necessary. Lay one piece of lining over the wadding and tuck the raw edges neatly between the wadding and the embroidery. Pin the layers in position and then slipstitch the lining neatly to the embroidery, using pink sewing thread. Repeat for the other side of the teacosy.

▢ Turn the teacosy to the right side and hand stitch the cording neatly around the edges as shown on the photograph.

MAKING CORDING

You can either use purchased cording or make your own, with lengths of pink perlé or crochet cotton. First twist strands together to decide how many strands you will need to make ¼in (6mm) diameter cording. To make 1½yd (1.3m) of cording, cut strands 4¾yd (4.1m) long. Put the strands together in one long bunch, with ends level. Tie the bunch in a knot at one end, and slip this end over a hook. Holding the other end of the bunch firmly, twist the strands tightly together. When the entire length is tightly twisted, place one finger at the center and bring the free ends level with the knotted ends. Remove your finger and the strands will twist into a cord. Trim

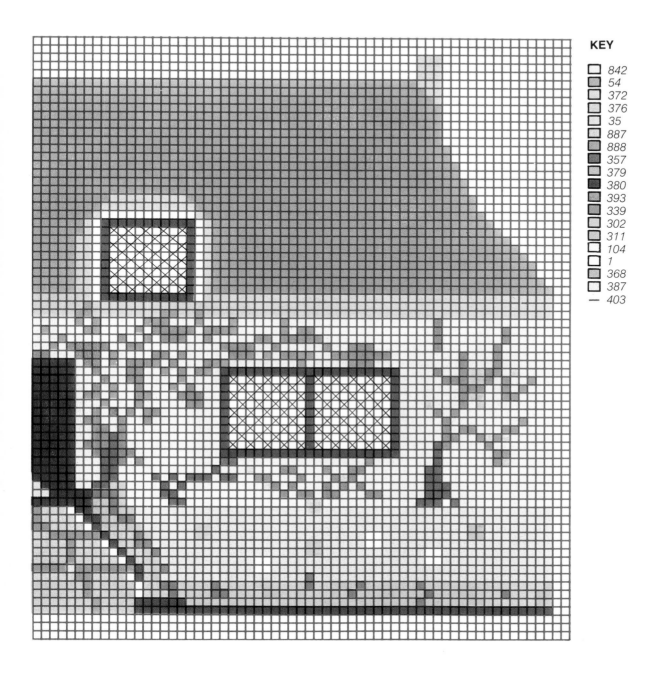

KEY

- 842
- 54
- 372
- 376
- 35
- 887
- 888
- 357
- 379
- 380
- 393
- 339
- 302
- 311
- 104
- 1
- 368
- 387
- — 403

away the first knot and knot all ends together. At the folded end of the cord, make another knot and trim the fold. If desired, use strands of different colors to produce multicolored cording.

SCATTERED FLOWERS

If you have an old or antique chair which you would like to recover, here is a charming way to do it with the minimum of effort for the maximum of effect: an easy-to-work needlepoint design which takes full advantage of the attractive, neutral tone and interesting texture of embroidery canvas and uses it as the background to a design of tiny, scattered flower sprays. Instead of spending hours and hours filling in a monotone background, you are left with the pleasant task of working the little flowers – if the idea wasn't so successful it would seem like cheating! The instructions explain how to remove the old covers and replace them with the finished needlepoint, though you may prefer to let a professional fit the new covers if you do not enjoy upholstery and you are afraid of spoiling the finished work.

Size: to the measure of your existing chair cover.

MATERIALS

Double-thread 10-gauge canvas: separate pieces for the front, back and seat of the chair
DMC tapestry wool in the following colors:
white *rose –* **gray** *7321, 7333;* **white**; **yellow** *7431 and 7745;* **orange** *7445;* **green** *7320, 7384*
pink *rose –* **yellow** *7431, 7786;* **pink** *7200, 7202, 7204;* **orange** *7445;* **green** *7362, 7382, 7542;* **white**
yellow *rose –* **orange** *7445;* **yellow** *7726, 7727;* **green** *7369, 7370, 7548, 7584;* **white***
(Quantities are not given as the amount required will vary according to your chair size and the spacing you choose to give between flowers.
Tapestry needle size 18 or 20
Tapestry frame – you could work without one, but a frame would make stitching easier and would help to prevent the canvas from becoming distorted
Cotton fabric (if undercover needs replacing)
⅜in (10mm) fine tacks
Two gimp pins
⅝in (1.5cm) wide braid
Curved upholstery needle
Matching thread
Fabric adhesive
Note *If the above yarns are unobtainable, refer to page 191.*

DIRECTIONS

▦ Using a wooden mallet and a ripping chisel, remove old back, front and seat covers, easing out old tacks and always working in the direction of the wood grain.
▦ If necessary, add more padding to the underneath and replace or renew undercover.
▦ Measure the seat both ways and buy canvas to this size, plus at least 8in (20cm) all around. Do the same for inside and outside back.

TAPESTRY

▦ To prevent fraying, bind the canvas edges with masking tape or turn under and stitch a narrow hem.
▦ The motifs are all worked in half cross stitch (see page 13) and each square represents one stitch. Embroider the motifs from the charts, using the photograph as a general guide to positioning. The background is unworked.
▦ As each piece is completed, stretch the canvas back into shape by blocking it: remove binding or holding stitches around edge and if there is a selvage cut small nicks along it to ensure the canvas can be stretched. Dampen the canvas with a wet sponge or a laundry spray.
▦ Take a piece of wood or

46

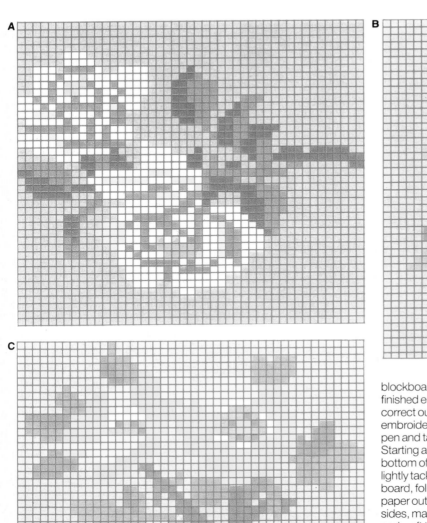

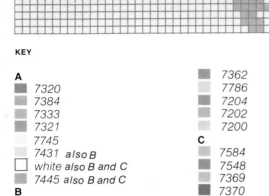

KEY

A

▮	7320
▮	7384
▮	7333
▮	7321
▮	7745
▮	7431 *also B*
☐	white *also B and C*
▮	7445 *also B and C*

B

▮	7542
▮	7382

▮	7362
▮	7786
▮	7204
▮	7202
▮	7200

C

▮	7584
▮	7548
▮	7369
▮	7370
▮	7726
▮	7727

blockboard larger than the finished embroidery, draw the correct outline of the completed embroidery with a waterproof pen and tape it to the board. Starting at the center top and bottom of the surplus canvas, lightly tack the canvas to the board, following the marked paper outline. Repeat at the sides, making sure that the warp and weft threads are at right angles. Hammer in tacks securely, then wet the canvas again and leave to dry slowly at room temperature over several days. Repeat as necessary until canvas is restored to shape.

THE COVERING

▦ Place the canvas over the seat and temporarily tack to front and side rails, stretching it taut. Smooth back edge down between back and seat and tack at back of chair to back rail.
▦ At front corners, pull side canvas around to the front rail and tack. Fold excess canvas at the front into a pleat in line with edge of seat (trimming off any excess canvas inside. Tack in place. Handstitch down the folded fabric at each front corner.

▦ Check that the seat is smooth and taut and hammer in the tacks.
▦ Center front canvas over chair back and temporarily tack to back of frame at top and sides. Pull lower edge through to the back of the chair and temporarily tack in place. At each side of top, excess canvas will have to be pleated up into small evenly spaced darts – make sure you have the same number of darts at each side. When the darts look right, hammer in the tacks.
▦ Cut the cotton fabric to fit outside back; centrally place over the back and tack in place inside previous row of tacks.
▦ Center the canvas over the cotton fabric on outside back, cutting and then turning under the top and side edges, following the lines of the chair and covering over previous tacks; pin in place. Secure lower edge with tacks. Using a curved needle, stitch the side and top edges to the inside back canvas.
▦ Cover tack heads at base with braid. Tack the end in place with a gimp pin, fold braid over tack and glue in place all around the base edge. Secure the opposite end with a gimp pin to finish.

COLOR AND LIGHT

Even in the middle of winter, this needlepoint mat will give you the feeling of warm sunshine pouring in through a stained glass window, illuminating an intricate pattern of bright, jewel-like colors. The dark outlines, like the leading in a window, enhance the colors until they seem to glow with life. Although the pattern is complex, it is worked on a large-scale canvas, which can be covered quickly.

Size: approximately 32in × 52in (80cm × 130cm).

MATERIALS

1⅛yd × 1⅝yd (1m × 1.5m) of 4-gauge DMC rug canvas
DMC rug wool (uncut) as follows: seven hanks of **gray** 7333; four hanks of **ecru**; two hanks each of **primrose** 7504, **blue** 7313 and **black**, and one hank each of **gold** 7505, **blue** 7301, 7305, 7307, 7317 and 7326, **pink** 7120, 7196, 7202 and 7206, **beige** 7491, **green** 7347, **sand** 7520, **bronze** 7421 and **tan** 7446 and 7444
Strong button thread
Large tapestry or rug needle
Fine-tip waterproof felt marker
Note If the above yarn is unobtainable, refer to page 191.

DIRECTIONS

▦ Draw a vertical line with the marker through the center of the canvas, taking care not to cross any vertical threads. Mark the central horizontal line in the same way. Rule the corresponding lines across the chart to find the center of the design.

▦ Bind the edges of the canvas with masking tape to prevent the threads unraveling. Begin stitching at the center of the canvas, working outwards and following the chart square by square. Each square on the chart represents one half cross stitch.

▦ Embroider the stained glass design first, and then work the black and gray border.

▦ Block the embroidery (see page 15) if it has pulled out of shape during stitching, then trim away the surplus canvas, leaving a margin of 2in (5cm) all around the embroidery.

▦ The rug can either be bound with strips of rug binding, as described on page 62, or finished as follows: cutting diagonally across, trim spare canvas from corners to reduce bulk. Fold the canvas to the back at each corner, then bring the side margins to the back to meet at a mitered fold.

▦ Using strong button thread, stitch the sides together along the mitered corners, then secure all edges to the back of the rug with herringbone stitch.

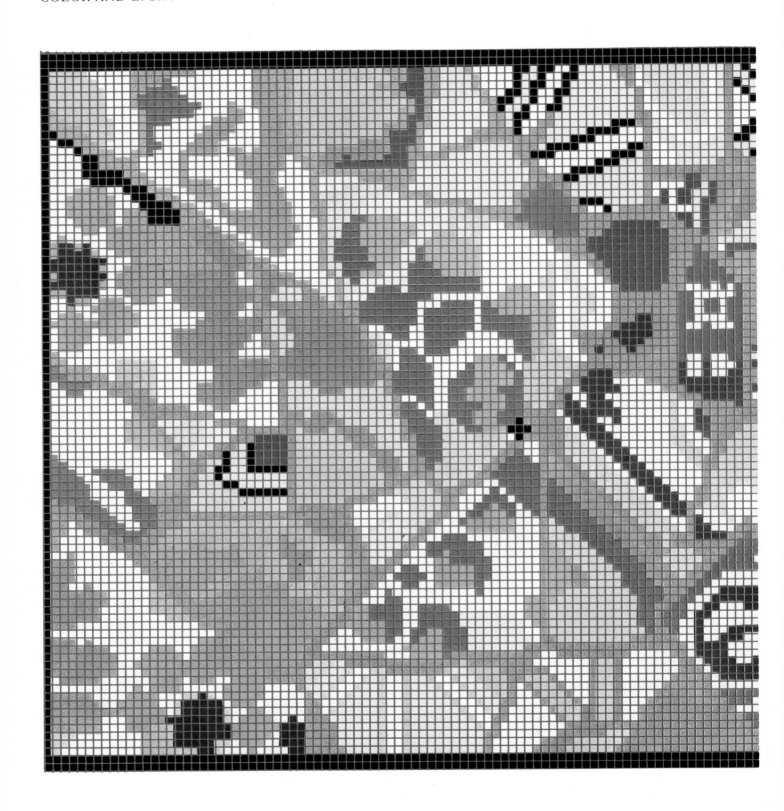

KEY

■	*black*
	7333
	7446
	7421
	7505
	7444
	7504
□	*ecru*
	7307
	7305
	7317
	7301
	7313
	7326
	7206
	7202
	7120
	7196
	7347
	7520
	7491

The pattern shows the central portion of the mat. In addition to the inner border of two rows of stitches in black, running all around the work, there is an outer border of gray, seven rows deep. The black inner border emphasizes the bright colors of the design and throws them into sharp relief, while the gray outer border suggests the stone walls which so often surround a stained glass window. If you wish to change the color of the outer border to match your surroundings, either make a tracing of the design and color it in, adding the borders, or shade strips of paper in the chosen border color and frame them around the design.

HOLIDAY SOUVENIRS

Practicality and beauty are combined in these two shopping bags, both of which are so pretty that they can be displayed on your kitchen wall when not in use. Alternatively, the designs could be used to make an attractive pair of cushion covers.

Size Each bag measures 15½in × 13in (39cm × 32.5cm).

MATERIALS

FOR ONE BAG
12in × 15in (24cm × 32cm) of single thread 12-gauge canvas
⅝yd (50cm) of 36in (90cm) wide strong linen or cotton fabric in a neutral color
Matching sewing thread

⅝yd (50cm) of 36in (90cm) wide lining fabric in a neutral color
Fine-point waterproof felt marker
Rectangular embroidery frame or stretcher
Tapestry needle size 20 or 22

Threads
SEASCAPE BAG
*DMC soft embroidery cotton: one skein each of **brown** 2400 and 2829, **gray** 2413, 2414, 2647 and 2933, **black** 2310, **blue** 2595 and 2807, **green** 2502, 2504, 2715 and 2926, and ochre 2575 and 2738, and two skeins each of **white**, **gray** 2415 and **green** 2928*

MOUNTAIN BAG
*DMC soft embroidery cotton: one skein each of **green** 2856, 2926 and 2928, **brown** 2801, **gray** 2233, 2931 and 2933, **beige** 2302, 2543 and 2842, **yellow** 2745, **cream** 2579, **ochre** 2833, and **red** 2304 and 2918, and two skeins each of **white** and **gray** 2415*

Embroidery Stitches
Both designs are worked in half cross stitch, each square representing one half cross stitch.

DIRECTIONS

THE EMBROIDERY
▣ Both pictures are stitched in the same way: start by drawing a vertical line with the felt marker down the center of the canvas rectangle, taking care not to cross any vertical threads. Mark the central horizontal line in the same way. Rule corresponding lines across the appropriate chart to find the center of the design.

▣ Mount the canvas in the embroidery frame or stretcher. Begin stitching the design at the center and work outwards in half cross stitch, following the appropriate chart square by square.

▣ When all the stitching is complete, block the canvas carefully, as explained on page 15.

MAKING THE BAG
▣ Cut out two pieces measuring 16¾in × 14¼in (42cm × 35.5cm) from the main fabric and two pieces the same size from the lining fabric. From main fabric only, cut two strips measuring 3in × 16in (7.5cm × 40cm).

▣ Take one main fabric piece for the front of the bag and, using a pencil, mark out a window for the picture, making it 1¼in (3cm) smaller each way than the dimensions of the embroidered area. The window should be an equal distance from the side and bottom edges of the fabric, and

slightly closer to the top edge.

■ Cut away the central portion of fabric and turn under an allowance of ⅝in (1.5cm) all around the opening, clipping into the corners so that the fabric will lie flat. Tack the turnings.

■ Position the fabric over the embroidery and tack in place. Machine stitch around the opening, close to the folded edge.

■ With right sides facing, pin bag front and back together and machine stitch them together along the sides and bottom edge, taking a ⅝in (1.5cm) seam allowance. Press the seam and turn the bag right side out. Stitch the lining sections together but do not turn them right side out.

■ Fold each handle strip in half lengthwise, with right sides facing, and machine down the long side, taking a ⅜in (1cm) seam allowance. Turn right side out and press.

■ Take one handle and position it on the front of the bag, with the raw ends of the handle matching the raw top edge of the bag. The ends should be in line with the side edges of the picture. Stitch across, taking a ⅝in (1.5cm) seam. Stitch the other handle to the back of the bag.

■ Bringing the handles up, turn under ⅝in (1.5cm) around the top edge of the bag and press. Machine stitch around the three seamed edges of the bag, stitching close to the edge. Turn under and press the raw top edge of the bag lining. Slip it into the bag, then pin and stitch the bag and lining together, machine stitching close to the folded edges.

MOUNTAINEER BAG

KEY

- 2856
- 2926
- 2928
- 2801
- 2233
- 2931
- 2933
- 2302
- 2543
- 2842
- 2745
- 2579
- 2833
- 2304
- 2918
- 2415
- white

SEASCAPE BAG

KEY

- 2400
- 2829
- 2413
- 2414
- 2933
- 2310
- 2595
- 2807
- 2502
- 2504
- 2715
- 2926
- 2575
- 2738
- white
- 2647
- 2415
- 2928

MAJOLICA MAT

A familiar image of the Mediterranean, blue-and-white tiles with their formal, often ornate, designs inspired this idea for a floor mat. Each square is worked separately mainly in cross stitch, then enriched with back stitch and Chinese knots to give the geometric precision of tiles. You have a wealth of designs here to make up as shown, or to adapt for your own ideas – table mats, cushions, chairbacks, folder covers, or a series of framed patterns. If you are ambitious, the mat itself could be enlarged by repeating a combination of the squares.

MATERIALS

20 squares of Pingouin rug canvas, each 20in (50cm) × 20in (50cm)	Large tapestry or rug needle

Threads
Pingouin rug wool: 40 hanks of **white** 05; 15 hanks of **blue** 67; 9 hanks of **blue** 31; 8 hanks of **blue** 65; 7 hanks of **blue** 40; 2 hanks of each of the following colors: **blue** 13, 32, 66, 134; 1 hank of **blue** 28

Embroidery Stitches
Cross stitch, back stitch, Chinese knots, herringbone stitch and half cross stitch.

DIRECTIONS

THE CHARTS:

▦ Use chart A for the four corner squares; charts B and C for the ten border squares that make up the garland, and charts 1, 2, 3 and 4 to make up the six central geometric squares: D, E, F, G.

▦ Embroider each square from the appropriate chart. Work squares A, B and C in cross stitch. Work the geometric squares in cross stitch and pick out extra details in back stitch and Chinese knots. Then embroider two rows of back stitch vertically and horizontally across the center of each square using colour 40.

▦ When all the squares have been embroidered, block each one carefully (see page 15), making sure that they are all the same size: each blocked square should measure 17in (40cm) × 16in (40cm).

▦ Following the arrangement in the diagram, join the squares into four strips of five squares with back stitched seams. Press the seams open.

▦ Join the strips together in the same way, making sure that the pattern is correct.

▦ On the reverse side of the rug, turn in the surplus canvas and secure it with herringbone stitch. Secure the surplus canvas along each seam in a similar way, using herring bone stitch.

▦ On the top side of the rug, use color 40 to conceal the seams – work rows of back stitch along them – and to finish the edges off work a row of half cross stitch round the outside of the rug.

Once you have mastered this rug, try using different 'tiles'.

This rug is made up of twenty sections of canvas work each measuring 16in (40cm) square. Embroider each of the sections systematically from the charts, beginning with the four corner squares which are worked from chart A. Charts B and C are followed to work the ten sections which complete the garland border. The border sections are worked in cross stitch.

The central portion of the rug is made up of six geometrically patterned sections worked in cross stitch, back stitch and Chinese knots. These sections are worked from charts 1, 2, 3 and 4 using different combinations of the pattern charts as shown in the plan.

There are various methods of making a rug non-slip. The simplest way is to coat the turned-under edges of the canvas with rubber-based adhesive and leave them to dry thoroughly.

A heavy lining also works well. Cut a piece of hessian slightly larger than the finished rug and turn under the raw edges. Slipstitch the hessian to the wrong side of the rug, as shown in the diagram.

Alternatively, non-slip netting can be purchased. This is cut slightly smaller than the rug and placed between it and the floor.

One section of the rug design can be worked and made into a cushion cover. Finish the edges in the same way as for the pansy bag (see page 40), and slipstitch it to a ready-made cushion cover.

This diagram shows the final arrangement of squares. The outer border is made up of fourteen squares (patterns A, B and C) and the six inner squares are composites, using the four small patterns opposite.

59

IKEBANA

This square rug, with its interplay of rich autumnal colors and rounded shapes, has a wonderful feeling of life and movement, like a split second taken from a juggling act. It was inspired by an antique Japanese textile, but its simple, almost abstract shapes would blend superbly into an uncluttered modern setting. If these colors are not suited to your decor, trace over the basic outlines and experiment with other colorways until you have found a combination that works. Even a very minor change, such as altering the color of some balls, perhaps to echo the color of a lamp base or some scatter cushions, could have a subtle but important effect, bringing the design into harmony with a room setting, without involving a great deal of extra preparation.

Size: approximately 55in × 55in (140cm × 140cm).

MATERIALS

60in × 60in (1.5m × 1.5m) of 4-gauge DMC rug canvas
DMC rug wool in ready-cut packs in the following quantities and colors: 85 packs **beige** 7143; 66 packs **fawn** 7520; 30 packs **black**; 24 packs red 7107; 19 packs **pale pink** 7120; 8 packs **green** 7384; 6 packs **orange** 7850; 5 packs **yellow** 7504; 4 packs **ecru**; 3 packs each of **blue** 7305 and **gold** 7505, and 2 packs of **pink** 7202
Latchet rug hook
Wide masking tape
6⅞yd (6.2m) of 1½in (4cm) wide rug binding
Heavy duty sewing needle
Beige button thread or linen carpet thread
Note If the above rug yarn is unobtainable, refer to page 191.

DIRECTIONS

▦ The rug is knotted using a latchet hook (see overleaf), and each square on the chart represents one rug knot worked over one horizontal thread of canvas.
▦ To make each knot, take a cut strand of wool and fold it in half. Holding the two ends firmly, slip the wool over the hook, below the crook and latch, and insert the hook under a horizontal thread of canvas.
▦ Open the latch and insert the two ends of wool into the hook then closing the latch, pull the ends back under the canvas thread and through the loop.
▦ Pull the two ends to make a firm knot before moving on to the next. If one side of a knot is longer than the other, do not be tempted to trim the longer end as this will

result in the finished rug having an uneven pile. Instead, remove the yarn and rework the knot.
▦ Before working the design, bind canvas edges with masking tape to prevent threads unraveling. Work row by row across the canvas, following chart for design and colors. Begin at the lower edge, approximately 4¾in (12cm) in from raw edge of canvas, and work upwards to top of chart, working in horizontal rows. Much of the background of the rug is worked in two colors in order to produce a more interesting, multicolored pile of either beige and fawn or beige and pink. It is important to stagger the position of the colors from row to row, rather like brickwork, in order to achieve a speckled effect instead of stripes.
▦ When knotting is complete, trim away surplus canvas, leaving

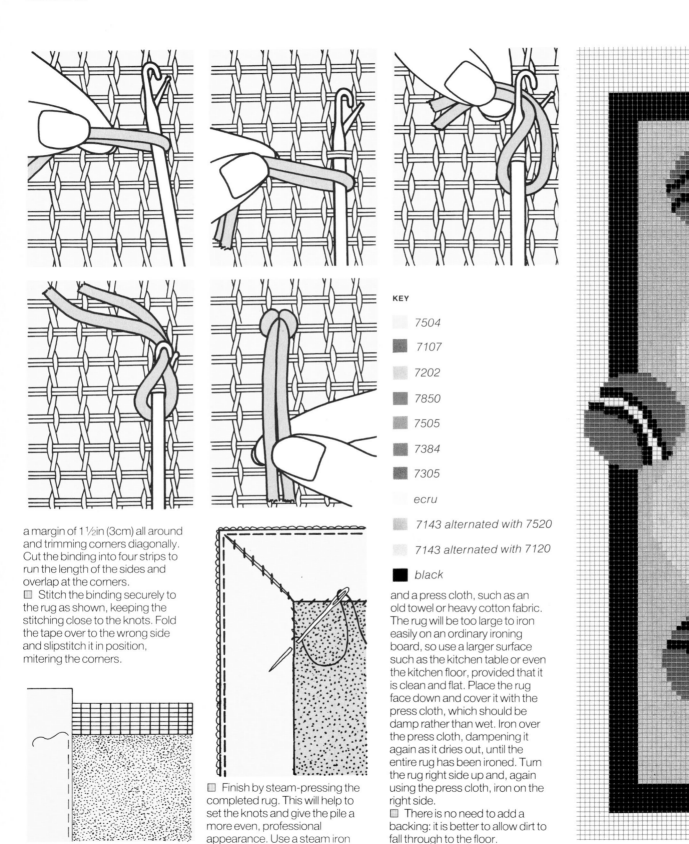

KEY

	7504
	7107
	7202
	7850
	7505
	7384
	7305
	ecru
	7143 alternated with 7520
	7143 alternated with 7120
■	*black*

a margin of 1½in (3cm) all around and trimming corners diagonally. Cut the binding into four strips to run the length of the sides and overlap at the corners.

▦ Stitch the binding securely to the rug as shown, keeping the stitching close to the knots. Fold the tape over to the wrong side and slipstitch it in position, mitering the corners.

▦ Finish by steam-pressing the completed rug. This will help to set the knots and give the pile a more even, professional appearance. Use a steam iron and a press cloth, such as an old towel or heavy cotton fabric. The rug will be too large to iron easily on an ordinary ironing board, so use a larger surface such as the kitchen table or even the kitchen floor, provided that it is clean and flat. Place the rug face down and cover it with the press cloth, which should be damp rather than wet. Iron over the press cloth, dampening it again as it dries out, until the entire rug has been ironed. Turn the rug right side up and, again using the press cloth, iron on the right side.

▦ There is no need to add a backing: it is better to allow dirt to fall through to the floor.

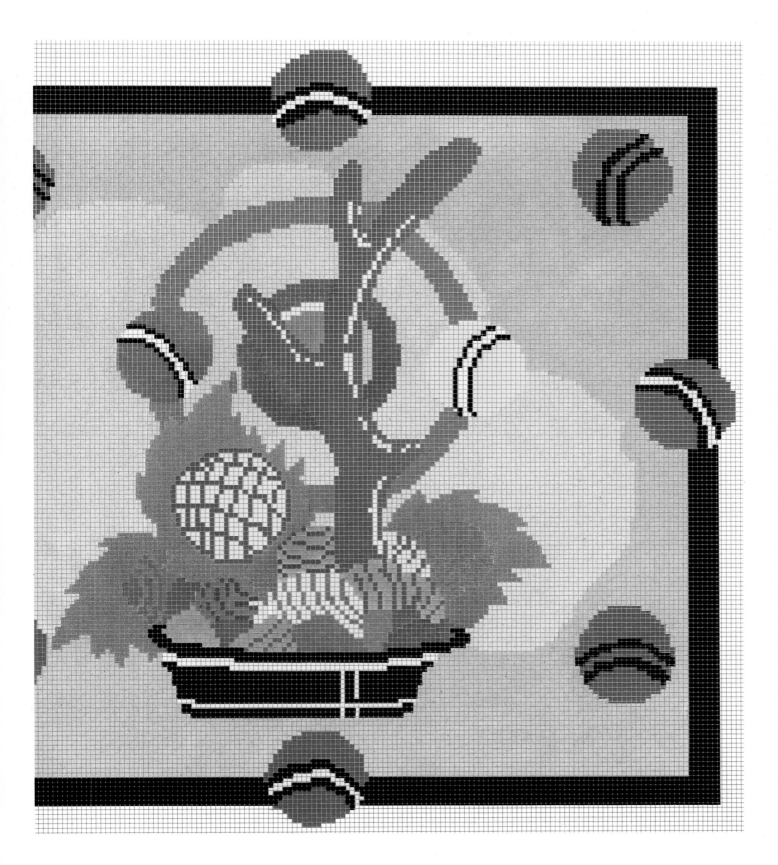

EMBROIDERY FOR YOU

ETHNIC FLOWERS

The brilliant colors of Hungarian floral embroidery have a timeless attraction. The beauty of these flowers is that you can be as ambitious or as small-scale as you like: a plain white dress can be made into a treasured object, or the motifs can be embroidered singly or in clusters for a bag, the front edges of a blouse, for the corner of a shawl or the point of a collar. And they are done simply and quickly in satin stitch and stem stitch. Vary the flower colors to your own taste, but keep them jewel-bright. As with the genuine article, a certain roughness in technique adds life.

MATERIALS

A ready-made garment, or fabric to be made into a shawl, tablecloth or cushion cover.

Crewel needle size 5 or 6
Embroidery hoop

Threads
DMC cotton perle no. 8 in the following shades:
SOLID COLORS: **green** 703, 704, 895; **yellow** 745, 973; **pink** 352, 818; **orange** 971; **red** 349, 606, 608, 817; **dark red** 815, 902, 3685; **purple** 550
SHADED COLOURS: **green** 122, 126; **blue** 113; **orange** 108; **pink** 99, 112; **red** 57; **mauve** 126

Embroidery Stitches
Satin stitch, stem stitch.

DIRECTIONS

▦ Transfer the chosen motifs to the fabric or garment using either the carbon paper method or the transfer pencil method given on page 11.
▦ Work with the fabric or garment stretched in an embroidery hoop, moving the hoop as necessary. If the fabric is very fine or delicate, protect it from damage with a piece of muslin (see page 10).
▦ Using the photograph and diagram on page 68 as color guides, embroider the flowers and leaves in satin stitch and the stems in stem stitch.
▦ When the embroidery is completed, place it face down on a well-padded surface and press lightly, taking care not to crush the stitches.

The flower motifs can be used to decorate other objects: a box lid (see page 122) or a handkerchief.

The floral designs are intended to be used in an individual way. Be as creative as you like: select single motifs and scatter them over the fabric; mass the flowers closely together to create the riot of color shown on the previous page; use use just one motif to highlight a garment.

CHORISTERS' COLLARS

These pretty collars in simple cross stitch are detachable, so they can be washed easily and worn with a variety of outfits. By choosing harmonious colors – gray and yellow, pink and blue, green and turquoise – you can make them to match any favorite dress or smock.

MATERIALS

For each design:
12in (30cm) × 15in (38cm) even-weave 18-gauge fabric, in white
White sewing thread

Crewel needle size 7 or 8
Sewing needle
5 pairs of small snap fasteners
1yd (1m) white cotton bias binding

Threads
DMC stranded cotton:
*1 strand of each: **yellow** 445;*
***gray** 318*

Embroidery Stitch
Cross stitch: each square on the charts represents one cross stitch worked over two horizontal and two vertical woven blocks of the fabric.

DIRECTIONS

▦ Enlarge the collar pattern to full size on plain paper from the measurements given (see page 10). Check the neckline of the dress to which the collar is to be attached against that of the pattern; adjust if necessary.

▦ Pin the pattern to the fabric and cut out the collar.

▦ Bind the neck edge of the collar with bias binding, as shown in the diagram. Then turn a double ³⁄₈in (1cm) hem around the remaining edges (see page 14 for instructions on mitering corners), pin and hand stitch. Press.

▦ Beginning ⁵⁄₈in (2cm) above the hem and working from the center front outwards, embroider the chosen design from the chart in cross stitch. Use three strands of thread throughout.

▦ When the embroidery is completed, place it face down on a well-padded surface and press lightly, taking care not to crush the stitches.

▦ Sew snap fasteners to the collar and dress, placing one pair of snaps at the center fronts, one on each shoulder line, and one at each side of the center-back opening.

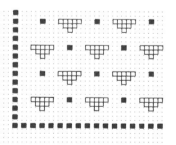

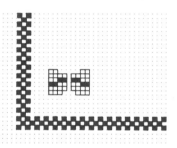

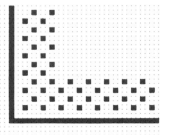

OAK LEAVES AND ACORNS

The couturier Schiaparelli loved creating surreal button designs and these oak leaves and acorns remind one of her inventiveness. Real acorns, threaded through with cord, make unusual buttons, and the acorn motifs embroidered around the buttonholes, on the cuffs, and on the lapels of the dark woolen blazer complement them perfectly.

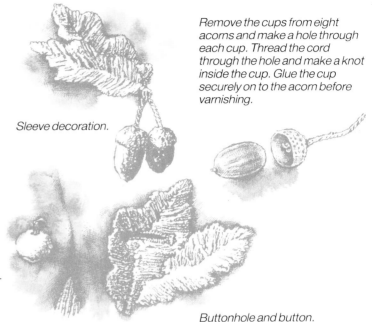

Sleeve decoration.

Remove the cups from eight acorns and make a hole through each cup. Thread the cord through the hole and make a knot inside the cup. Glue the cup securely on to the acorn before varnishing.

MATERIALS

Ready-made woolen jacket with a fairly smooth weave	Card
16 acorns with cups	Polyurethane varnish
8 short lengths of thin cord in matching or contrasting colors to the embroidery threads	Small paintbrush
	Glue
	White dress marking chalk
	Crewel needle size 3 or 4
	Large chenille needle

Threads
DMC stranded cotton:
pale green 368; **dull gold** 834

Embroidery Stitch
Satin stitch.

Buttonhole and button.

DIRECTIONS

▦ To prepare the acorn 'buttons' thread short lengths of cord through eight acorns, as shown in the diagrams. Remove the cups from the remaining acorns and make a hole through each one as shown. Using a small paintbrush, seal the acorns with the varnish and hang them up to dry; allow twenty-four hours for the varnish to dry thoroughly.

▦ Trace the leaf shapes and transfer them to card. Make a set of templates by carefully cutting round each leaf with a sharp pair of scissors. Using the photographs as a guide, position the templates on the jacket – on the lapels, the edge of the sleeves and round each of the buttonholes – and draw round them with a dress marking chalk.

▦ Embroider the leaves in satin stitch using six strands of thread, taking care to cover the guide lines.

▦ Attach the acorn 'buttons' opposite the buttonholes.

▦ Thread each cord of the other set of acorns through the large chenille needle, pull the cords through to the reverse of the jacket and knot each one securely.

PERENNIAL PLEASURES

This rich anemone spray adds individuality and color to a simple classic sweater. Much easier to achieve than it at first appears, the embroidery is worked on a small piece of fine cotton and then appliquéd onto the sweater in a cunning method that makes the joining invisible. You could stitch a floral spray like this – perhaps scaled down – to attach to a velvet or silk cummerbund, to the back of a kimono or a light jacket.

MATERIALS

Ready-made round-necked cotton sweater in pink (the sweater should be of a medium weight to support the embroidery adequately).

16in (40cm) × 12in (30cm) fine white cotton fabric.
Crewel needle size 4 or 5
Embroidery hoop

Threads
DMC stranded cotton:
2 skeins of each of the following colors: SOLID COLORS: **pink** 600, 601, 602, 603, 604, 605, 754, 818, 819, 948; **yellow** 3078; **green** 320, 730, 734; **red** 606, 666, 815; **blue** 793; **mauve** 554
SHADED COLORS: **blue** 67, 121, 124; **pink** 48, 62, 112; **mauve** 52, 95, 99, 126; **green** 92, 94

Embroidery Stitch
Long and short stitch with a stitch length of approximately ⅛ to ³⁄₁₆ (3 to 4mm).

DIRECTIONS

▣ Enlarge the design to the measurements given on the pattern (see page 10). Transfer the design to the fine white cotton using one of the methods given on page 11.
▣ Work with the fabric stretched in an embroidery hoop, moving the hoop as necessary.
▣ Using the photograph and diagram as color guides, embroider the flowers and leaves in long and short stitch, but leave a narrow area the width of one row of stitches inside the edge of the design. Work with six strands of thread throughout.
▣ When the embroidery is completed apart from the border strip, place it face down on a well-padded surface and press lightly, taking care not to crush the stitches.
▣ Cut away the surplus fabric with a sharp pair of scissors.

▣ Tack the embroidery in place on the sweater. Then work the border strip in long and short stitch, taking the stitches through both the fabric and the jumper and keeping them close together so that the fabric edge is completely covered.

Place the embroidery over the right shoulder as shown.

To make the belt shown in the picture above, cut a length of belt stiffening to the correct size and place centrally to the wrong side of the embroidery. Fold the edges of the embroidered fabric over the stiffening, making neat corners. Cut a length of lining to the correct size plus ⅝in (1.5cm) all round. Turn in all edges and handstitch to wrong side of belt. Handstitch ribbon centrally to right side.

The design overlaps by ⅜in (1cm) at the center. Trace the two sections and overlap the tracings to get the complete pattern.

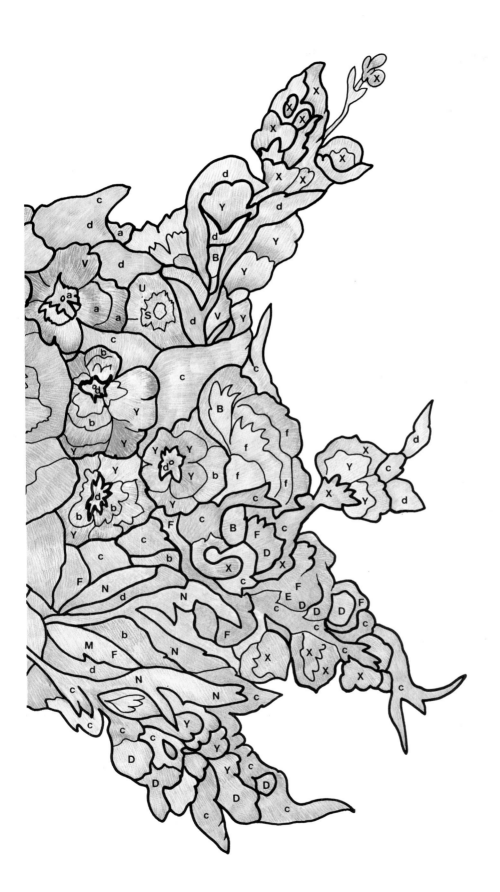

KEY

A	600
B	601
C	602
D	603
E	604
F	605
G	754
H	818
I	819
J	948
K	3078
L	320
M	730
N	734
P	666
Q	815
R	793
S	554
T	67
U	121
V	124
W	48
X	62
Y	112
Z	107
a	52
b	126
c	92
d	94
e	95
f	106
g	606
h	99

The thicker outlines on the design indicate the main shapes, with the thin lines detailing the shading of the interlocking long and short stitches.

The colored areas on the design will act as a guide to the threads, but refer to the key shown above for the accurate thread numbers.

A POCKETFUL OF FLOWERS

Choose any well-made blouse or shirt and work a little magic to make a flower spray blossom from the pocket. Honeysuckle, bluebells and violets all trail prettily and are simple to embroider.

MATERIALS

Ready-made shirt with a plain patch pocket on the chest 10in (25cm) × 10in (25cm) muslin or fine cotton (if shirt fabric is fine or delicate) Crewel needles sizes 4, 6 and 8 Embroidery hoop

Thread
DMC stranded embroidery cotton in the following shades:
FOR THE BLUEBELLS 1 skein of each:
blue 322, 798, 800, 813; **green** 368, 369, 502, 504, 966, 989; **pink** 224, 842; **yellow** 734
FOR THE HONEYSUCKLE 1 skein of each:
green 368, 704, 988, 989; **yellow** 725, 781, 783, 3078; **pink** 225, 316, 356, 739, 758, 760
FOR THE VIOLETS 1 skein of each:
green 368, 937, 966, 988, 989; **mauve** and **pink** 224, 225, 315, 316, 778; **yellow** 726

Embroidery Stitches
BLUEBELLS: long and short stitch, satin stitch, stem stitch, straight stitch.
HONEYSUCKLE: long and short stitch, satin stitch, stem stitch, Chinese knots.
VIOLETS: long and short stitch, satin stitch and stem stitch.

DIRECTIONS

▦ Transfer the design to the front of the shirt by either the carbon paper or transfer pencil method given on page 11 and positioning it as shown in the photographs. Transfer a single flower to the top of the adjacent sleeve.

▦ If the fabric to be embroidered is fine or delicate, work with both the shirt and the muslin (or cotton) stretched in an embroidery hoop. Cut away the central portion of the muslin to expose the area to be worked. Repeat with a second square of muslin if the design will not fit completely into the hoop, and the hoop needs to be moved.

▦ When working the embroidery use the photographs and diagrams as color guides.

▦ FOR THE BLUEBELLS, embroider the flowers and leaves in long and short stitch, using satin stitch for the narrow areas. Work the stems of the bluebells and the background foliage in stem stitch, adding groups of straight stitches in pink. Use two strands of thread throughout.

▦ FOR THE HONEYSUCKLE, embroider the flowers and leaves in long and short stitch, using satin stitch for the narrow areas. Work the stems and stamens in stem stitch, and the pistils and pollen in Chinese knots. Use two strands of thread for the flowers, leaves and stems; one strand for the stamens; three strands for the pollen, and six strands for the pistils.

▦ FOR THE VIOLETS, embroider the flowers and leaves in long and short stitch, using satin stitch for the flower centers. Work the stems and leaf veins in stem stitch. Use two strands of thread throughout.

▦ When the embroidery is completed place the shirt face down on a well-padded surface and press lightly, taking care not to crush the stitches.

Bluebell
a 798, **b** 800, **c** 813, **d** 322,
e 989, **f** 966, **g** 502, **h** 504,
i 368, **j** 369, **k** 842, **l** 224, **m** 734

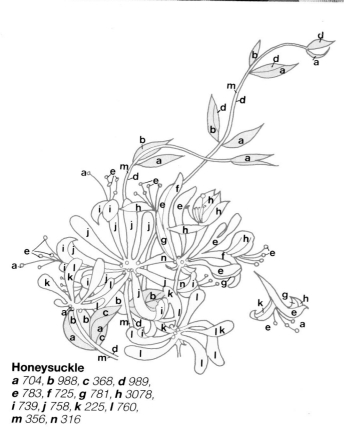

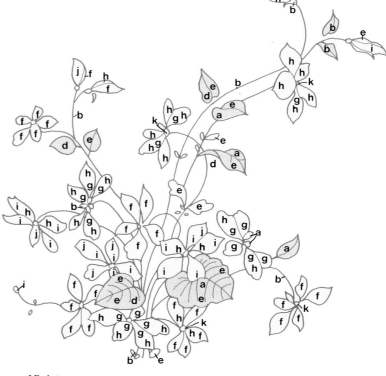

Honeysuckle
a 704, *b* 988, *c* 368, *d* 989,
e 783, *f* 725, *g* 781, *h* 3078,
i 739, *j* 758, *k* 225, *l* 760,
m 356, *n* 316

Violet
a 368, *b* 966, *c* 937, *d* 988,
e 989, *f* 224, *g* 315, *h* 316,
i 778, *j* 225, *k* 726

JUICY FRUITS

Clusters of strawberries or cherries are a perfect decoration for summer whites and pastels – for a dress yoke, a pretty sash or bow, for collars, cuffs, and hemlines. Satin stitch and Chinese knots are quick to embroider and brighten up all sorts of modest everyday objects, such as a tablecloth and napkins or plain kitchen curtains.

MATERIALS

Ribbon and ready-made garment, or household linen	*Crewel needle size 4 or 5* *Embroidery hoop*

Threads
DMC stranded cotton:
THE STRAWBERRIES: **red** *309;*
green *911, 954*
THE CHERRIES: **red** *321;* **green** *909*

Embroidery Stitches
Satin stitch, Chinese knots.

DIRECTIONS

▦ Transfer the design to the fabric using one of the methods given on page 11.
▦ Work with the fabric stretched in an embroidery hoop.
▦ Embroider the strawberries and leaves in satin stitch using the red and darker green threads, then scatter Chinese knots in the lighter green over the strawberries. Use six strands of thread throughout.
▦ Embroider the cherries, stalks and leaves in satin stitch, using six strands of thread throughout.
▦ When the embroidery is completed, place it face down on a well-padded surface and press lightly, taking care not to crush the stitches.

Embroider these strawberry and cherry motifs to add a touch of summer to clothes and household linen. They look best worked on a white or pale-colored background to show off the bright red and green of the threads. Use them singly, scattered at random, or in neat rows to make an unusual border pattern.

To place the strawberries in the correct position, first tie the ribbon into the desired shape bow. Then mark where the strawberries would look best on the ribbon. Untie the ribbon carefully and mark out the design and embroider it.

BABY ALPHABET

Straight out of Kate Greenaway, this alphabet layette will be a childhood treasure. The skilled embroiderer can make a quilt for the cot; those less patient could use the appropriate initials to add a little color and individuality to the simplest baby clothes. The letters are formed in padded satin stitch, while the charming figures are easy to copy in long and short stitch. Use pillow cases or quilt covers if you prefer, but remember wadded fabric will not fit into your embroidery hoop.

MATERIALS

1yd (1m) × 1yd (1m) of white cotton or linen for the cover	*pillowcase*
Ready-made baby cotton or linen	*Crewel needle size 6 or 7*
	Embroidery hoop

Threads
DMC stranded cotton (the colors are given below each diagram and are the ones used for the alphabet in the photograph, but you could substitute other colors if you prefer)
MAIN PART OF LETTERS: **turquoise** *807*
FACES, ARMS AND LEGS: **flesh pink** *754*
CHEEKS: **pink** *761*

Embroidery Stitches
Padded satin stitch, back stitch, horizontal long and short stitch, straight stitch.

DIRECTIONS

 Enlarge the design to the desired dimension. Transfer the complete alphabet to the square of white fabric using one of the methods given on page 11 and center it. Transfer two letters to the top corners of the pillowcase, using the photograph as a guide to the placement.

 Using the close-up photographs as a guide to the way stitches are used and the diagrams as color guides, embroider the letters in padded satin stitch with back stitch for the narrow areas. Embroider the figures in horizontal long and short stitch, with straight stitch and back stitch for the outlines, stripes and tiny details. Work with three strands of thread throughout.

 When the embroidery is completed, place it face down on a well-padded surface and press lightly, taking care not to crush the stitches.

 Turn a narrow hem round the cot cover (see page 14 for instructions on mitering corners) and machine or hand stitch.

Embroider the letters first and then the solid areas of the figures. Lastly, pick out the outlines, stripes and tiny details to give definition.

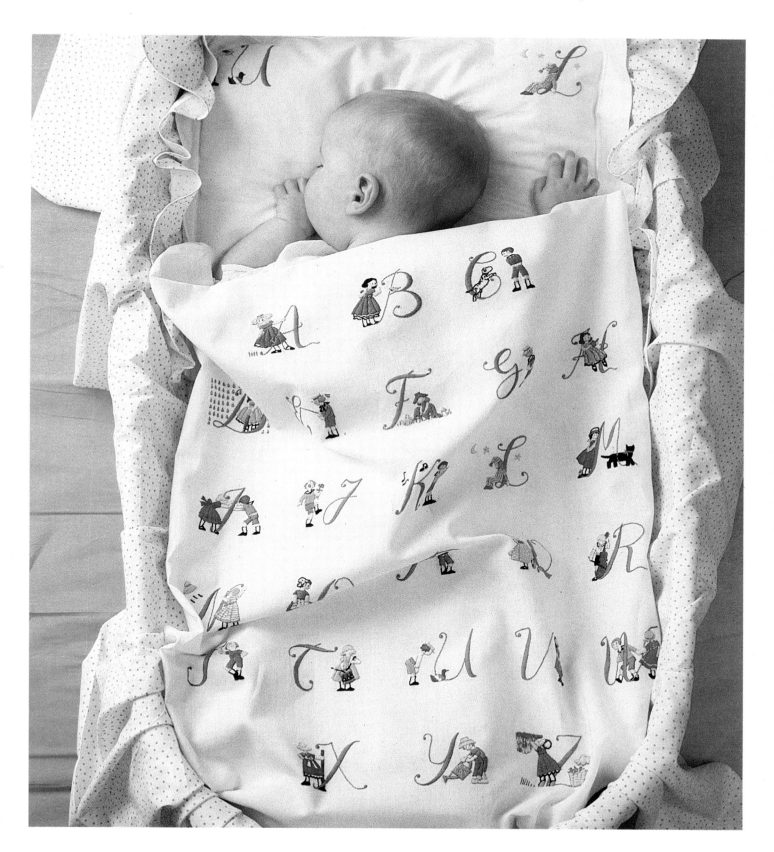

LETTER A: **pink** 957, **yellow** 726, **green** 320, **pink** 3350, **black** 310, **purple** 208

LETTER B: **black** 310, **pink** 3350, **green** 912, **yellow** 726, **blue** 927, **red** 321

LETTER C: **black** 310, **red** 321, **brown** 400, **blue** 826, **purple** 208, **pink** 957

LETTER D: **blue** 927, **brown** 400, **purple** 208, **pink** 957, 3350, **gold** 783, **black** 310

LETTER I: **purple** 208, **turquoise** 806, **yellow** 726, **black** 310, **brown** 400, **pink** 3350, **coral** 351, **green** 954, 320

LETTER J: **tan** 976, **black** 310, **green** 954, **blue** 826, **red** 350

LETTER K: **black** 310, **brown** 400, **tan** 976, **pink** 957, 3350, **blue** 826

LETTER L: **red** 350, **turquoise** 807, **blue** 828, **tan** 976, **yellow** 726

LETTER O: **blue** 826, 828, **brown** 400, **pink** 3350, **flesh pink** 754, **blue** 927, **yellow** 725, **black** 310

LETTER P: **black** 310, **blue** 826, **purple** 208

LETTER Q: **blue** 826, **pink** 957, **gold** 783, **fawn** 613, **black** 310, **white**

LETTER R: **yellow** 726, **green** 954, **brown** 400, **black** 310, **cream** 712

LETTER U: **brown** 400, **coral** 351, **yellow** 725, **cream** 712, **black** 310, **blue** 930, **green** 912, 954

LETTER V: **yellow** 726, **red** 320, **black** 310, **blue** 826, **pink** 3350

LETTER W: **tan** 976, **green** 954, **pink** 957, 3350, **black** 310, **purple** 208

LETTER X: **yellow** 726, **blue** 826, **pink** 3350, **brown** 400, **white**

LETTER E: **red** 321, 350, **blue** 828, **black** 310, **tan** 976, **green** 912, **gold** 783, **yellow** 726

LETTER F: **pink** 3350, **blue** 826, **tan** 976, **yellow** 725, 726, **green** 320, **fawn** 613, **cream** 712, **black** 310

LETTER G: **yellow** 726, **red** 350, **gold** 783, **purple** 208, **fawn** 613, **black** 310

LETTER H: **brown** 400, **red** 350, **pink** 3350, **green** 954, **black** 310, **white**

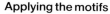

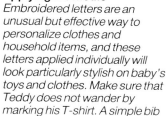

LETTER M: **pink** 3350, **black** 310, **purple** 208, **blue** 826

LETTER N: **yellow** 725, 726, **coral** 351, **black** 310, **green** 954, **gold** 783, **white**

Applying the motifs

Embroidered letters are an unusual but effective way to personalize clothes and household items, and these letters applied individually will look particularly stylish on baby's toys and clothes. Make sure that Teddy does not wander by marking his T-shirt. A simple bib or baby suit can be given a touch of individuality with the first letter of the owner's name embroidered in a prominent place. And, if you do not have the time to embroider the complete alphabet on a baby quilt, simply embroider baby's name or initials.

LETTER S: **tan** 976, **purple** 208, **red** 350, **black** 310, **turquoise** 806

LETTER T: **black** 310, **red** 321, **green** 954, **pink** 957, **yellow** 726, **blue** 826, **cream** 712

LETTER Y: **yellow** 725, **gold** 783, **coral** 351, **blue** 826, 927, **purple** 208

LETTER Z: **yellow** 725, 726, **red** 321, **green** 320, 369, **turquoise** 806, **black** 310, **purple** 208, **gold** 783, **brown** 400

BEETLE BACKS

Little monsters with shiny exotic wings are a wittier decoration to wear on your sleeve than a tender heart! They look all the better for advancing in a cluster: simple satin and straight stitch make them easy to embroider. The designs were copied straight from a book on insects – why not explore studies on fauna for some other unusual motifs? With luck you can find a subject just the right size and trace directly over it for your transfer.

MATERIALS

Ready-made white cotton shirt with short sleeves	Small piece of stiff card
Crewel needle size 7 or 8	Embroidery hoop

Threads
DMC stranded cotton as indicated below each beetle.

Embroidery Stitches
Satin stitch, straight stitch.

DIRECTIONS

 Enlarge the designs to the desired dimension. Place the piece of card in the sleeve to protect the under-sleeve and transfer the design to the fabric using the carbon paper method given on page 11. Then remove the card.

▦ Work with the fabric stretched in an embroidery hoop, moving the hoop as necessary.

▦ Using the photographs and diagrams as color guides, embroider each beetle body in satin stitch and the antennae and narrow parts of the legs in straight stitch. Use two strands of threads throughout.

▦ When the embroidery is completed, place it face down on a well-padded surface and press lightly, taking care not to crush the stitches.

BEETLE 1: **yellow** 742, 747; **green** 943, 991; **blue** 807

BEETLE 2: **yellow** 307, 726; **ocher** 783; **brown** 434; **black** 310

BEETLE 3: **red** 355; **green** 943, 991; **brown** 301; **ocher** 783

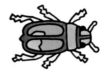

BEETLE 4: **green** 704, 943, 991; **yellow** 727; **brown** 801

BEETLE 5: **yellow** 744, 783; **black** 310; **chestnut** 976

BEETLE 6: **yellow** 472; **black** 310; **ocher** 729

BEETLE 7: **red** 666; **black** 310; **yellow** 727

BEETLE 8: **orange** 741; **brown** 3371; **red** 349; **ocher** 729

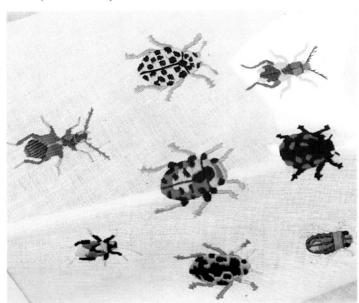

a surprise from nature's sketch-book

EMBROIDERY FOR YOUR HOME

STRAWBERRY FAIR

Tendrils of wild strawberries make a perfect border for a white tablecloth, set for summer. They have the restrained prettiness of an Edwardian, hand-painted watercolor. Chinese knots are used for the berry seeds over satin stitch, in subtle blends of color.

MATERIALS

One plain white tablecloth with a fine, smooth weave, preferably in pure cotton. If a square cloth is used it should measure at least 5ft 6in (165cm) across to allow for one complete spray to be worked along each side. If you prefer a rectangular cloth, the length should be at least 4ft 6in (137cm) to accommodate one complete spray along each long side. Crewel needle size 7 or 8. Embroidery hoop

Threads
DMC stranded cotton
Flowers: **pink** *819, 3689;* **gold** *676;* **green** *954*
Strawberries: **red** *321, 498, 815;* **white**
LEAVES 1: **green** *367, 989; veins –* **green** *319*
LEAVES 2: **gold** *834;* **green** *3013; veins –* **dull green** *3053*

Embroidery Stitches
Long and short stitch, encroaching satin stitch, satin stitch, Chinese knots, stem stitch.

DIRECTIONS

▦ Enlarge the design on page 90 to the measurements given on the pattern. Transfer it to the cloth using one of the methods given on page 11.

▦ Work with the cloth stretched in an embroidery hoop, moving the hoop along the cloth as each portion is completed, and use three strands of the thread.

▦ To embroider the flowers, work one row of long and short stitch in the deep pink along the edge of the petals. Fill in the petals using the light pink and the same stitch until the center circle is reached.

▦ Mass Chinese knots in yellow to make the raised center and work the small leaves between the petals in green satin stitch.

▦ Embroider the strawberries in encroaching satin stitch in three shades of red: use the darkest red to outline the shape, and then fill in towards the center, shading the fruit from dark to light.

▦ Scatter tiny white Chinese knots over this stitching.

▦ Work the calyx in satin stitch using either green or gold, as shown on the pattern.

▦ Embroider the leaves in shades of green (leaves 1) or gold (leaves 2), as indicated on the pattern. Work a row of encroaching satin stitch in the darker color round the edge of the leaf and then fill in the remainder using the same stitch and the lighter color.

▦ Work the veins in stem stitch.

▦ Embroider the stalks in stem stitch using one strand of each green used on leaf 1 to make up a three-strand thread.

▦ When the embroidery is complete, place the cloth face down on a well-padded surface and press lightly, taking care not to crush the stitches.

The flower and strawberry are shown life-size. Use them as a guide for blending the colors from dark to light. They also show the stitches which are used for each motif.

Use the leaf diagrams as a guide
to blending the different colors
of encroaching satin stitch. Leaf 1
is in three shades of green and
leaf 2 is in green mixed with gold

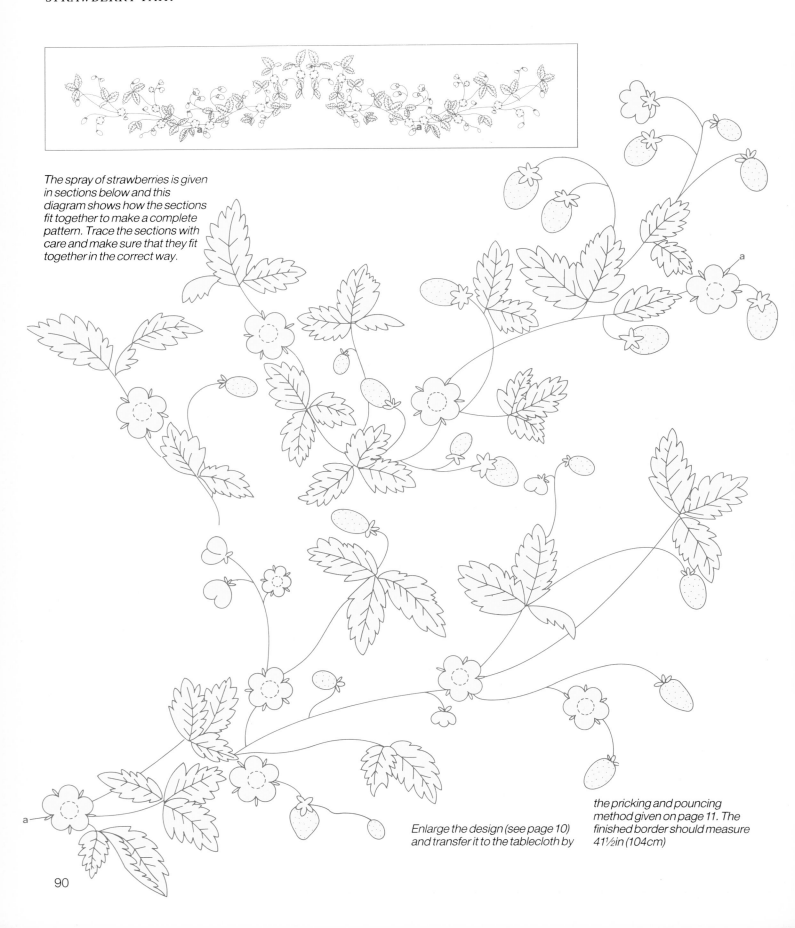

The spray of strawberries is given in sections below and this diagram shows how the sections fit together to make a complete pattern. Trace the sections with care and make sure that they fit together in the correct way.

Enlarge the design (see page 10) and transfer it to the tablecloth by the pricking and pouncing method given on page 11. The finished border should measure 41½in (104cm)

RUG TRANSFORMATION

If you are looking for something to brighten a corner of your room without going to enormous effort or expense, here is a comparatively quick way of adding your personal touch to a plain rug or mat and transforming it with a trelliswork and some scattered flowers. This simple pattern can easily be adapted to any size of rug, either by altering the scale or by simply extending the trellis in either direction, perhaps adding more random flowers.

Size: approximately 40in × 76in (100cm × 190cm) for quantities given.

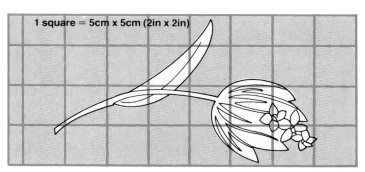

1 square = 5cm x 5cm (2in x 2in)

MATERIALS

Woven rug in cotton or wool
Pingouin yarns in the following quantities and colors: Iceberg —two balls **yellow** 473 and one ball **black** 41; Pingostar—two balls **gray** 512 and one ball **dark blue** 528; Pingoland—one ball each of **dark pink** 822 and **red** 831; Tapis—one ball each of **kingfisher** 60 and **emerald** 35;

Comfortable sport—one ball **bright pink** 33
Large chenille needle
Tracing paper
Dressmakers' carbon paper
8in × 40in (20cm × 1m) strip of stiff card
Fine-tipped waterproof felt marker

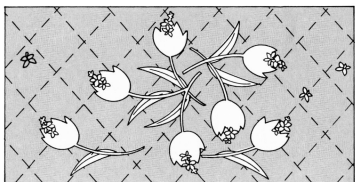

DIRECTIONS

▢ On reverse side of rug, mark a trellis of diagonal lines 8in (20cm) apart with the marker, using the strip of card as a guide.

▢ Enlarge the single flower pattern on tracing paper and, using dressmakers' carbon paper and turning the flower tracing different ways, transfer the complete pattern of scattered flowers to the right side of the rug.

▢ Embroider the flowers and leaves in long and short stitch and the gray stems and black pistils in overcast stitch as shown below, using the photograph as a color and stitch guide.

▢ Following the lines marked on the reverse of the rug, embroider the diagonal black lines in darning stitch, keeping each stitch approximately ⅜in (1cm) long.

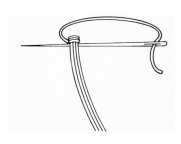

CYPRESS, PALM AND PINE

Embroidered pictures so often look ornate and out of keeping with modern interiors. But these tree specimens have the delicacy of botanical prints, burnished with a southern sunset. Use a fine, sand-colored linen as a harmonious background, and mount the studies simply between sheets of plastic.

MATERIALS

22in (55cm) × 22in (55cm) linen or cotton fabric in a neutral color for each tree	Crewel needle size 6 or 7 Large embroidery hoop

Threads
DMC stranded cotton – 1 skein in each of the following colors:
THE PALM TREE: **brown** 433, 938, 3045; **green** 470, 472, 500, 890, 987
THE CYPRESS TREE: **brown** 940, 3032, 3371; **mauve** 413; **green** 500, 502, 503, 504, 924
THE PINE TREE: **green** 500, 580, 732, 937

Embroidery Stitches
PALM TREE: satin stitch, straight stitch, long and short stitch.
CYPRESS AND PINE TREES: long and short stitch.

DIRECTIONS

▦ Enlarge the design to the measurements given on the pattern. Transfer the design to the fabric using one of the methods given on page 11.
▦ Work with the fabric stretched in a large embroidery hoop, moving the hoop as necessary.
▦ Using the diagrams as a color guide, embroider the palm tree in satin stitch and long and short stitch for the trunk, and straight stitch for the fronds. Using the close-up photograph as a guide, embroider the cypress and pine trees in long and short stitch. Use three strands of thread throughout.
▦ When the embroidery is completed, place it face down on a well-padded surface and press lightly, taking care not to crush the stitches.
▦ The pictures can be framed with a conventional frame, or mounted very simply between two sheets of plastic as shown in the photograph.

Frame the embroidery between two sheets of plastic clipped together. A small strip of double-sided tape can be used on the back of each corner to hold the embroidery in place.

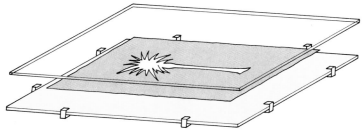

Cypress
a *504*
b *503*
c *502*
d *924*
e *413*
f *500*
g *3371*
h *840*
i *3032*

Palm
a *472*
b *987*
c *470*
d *890*
e *500*
f *433*
g *938*
h *3045*

Pine
a *732*
b *580*
c *937*
d *500*
e *938*
f *869*
g *780*
h *434*

TROPICAL PARADISE

Size 56in × 56in (144cm × 144cm).

MATERIALS

1⅝yd × 1⅝yd (1.5m × 1.5m) of black cotton or cotton/linen fabric (the motifs are placed at random, so it does not matter if you choose to change the dimensions slightly)

Black sewing thread
Crewel needle size 3 or 4
Dressmakers' carbon paper in a light color
Large embroidery hoop

Threads
DMC Soft Embroidery Cotton: one skein each of **yellow** 2741 and 2743, **blue** 2597, 2599, 2797, 2798 and 2807, **gray** 2415, **green** 2347, 2595, 2788, 2952, 2954, 2956, 2957, 2905 and 2909, **orange** 2740, 2742, 2946 and 2947, **pink** 2351 and 2892, **red** 2349, **violet** 2209, **brown** 2299 and 2839, and two skeins each of **yellow** 2307 and 2745, **blue** 2826, and **gray** 2318

Embroidery stitches
Encroaching satin stitch, straight stitch, stem stitch and Chinese knots.

13

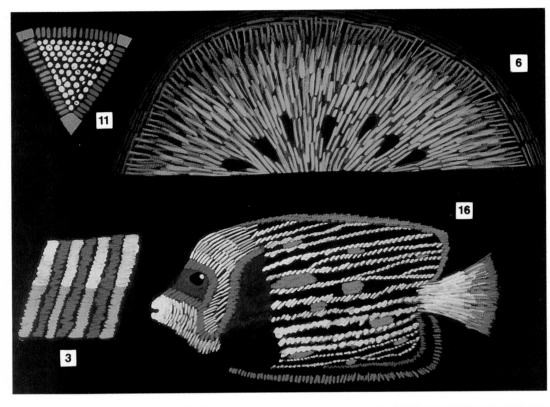

DIRECTIONS

▦ Trace the outlines of the motifs, all of which are shown half size, and enlarge them to the required dimensions, as shown on page 10. You will probably find it easier to fill in the minor details by hand, or to 'paint' them directly with your needle.

▦ Using the photograph as a general guide to position, transfer the outlines to the fabric, using dressmakers' carbon paper.

▦ Work with the fabric stretched in the embroidery hoop and re-position it as necessary. Embroider the motifs, using the photographs as stitch and color guides.

▦ When the embroidery is completed, place the fabric face down on a well-padded surface and press it lightly, taking care not to crush the stitches.

▦ Turn under a double ⅝in (1.5cm) hem along each edge of the square of fabric, mitering the corners, and hem by hand. Press the hem.

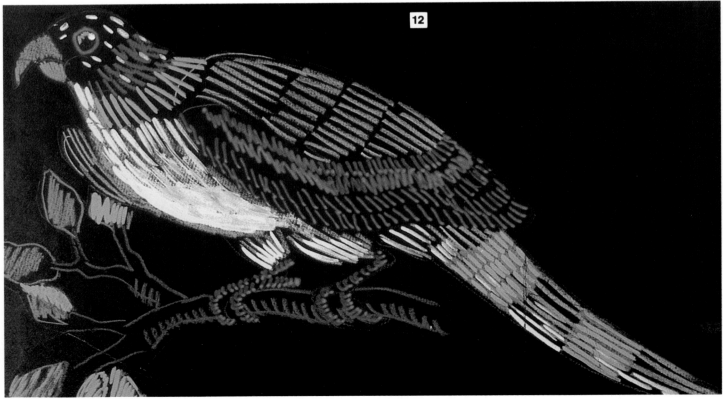

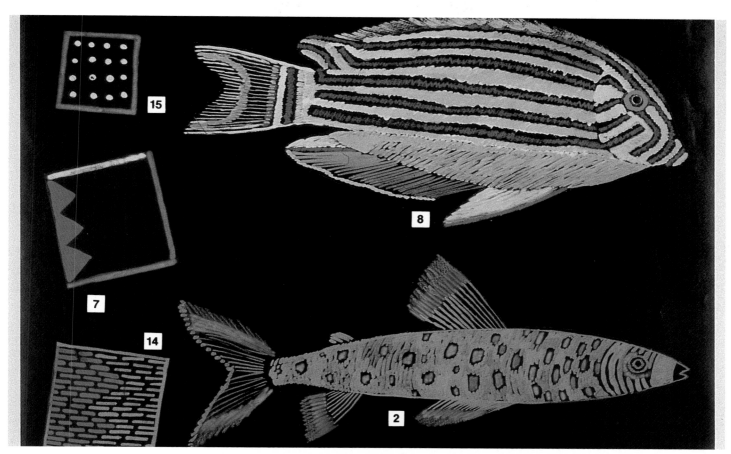

Colours used for each motif
1 2307 and 2956
2 2318, 2946 and 2347
3 2743, 2741 and 2826
4 2798 and 2957
5 2743, 2954 and 2351
6 2892, 2351, 2595, 2952 and
  2954
7 2349 and 2892
8 2742, 2741, 2743, 2788, 2826,
  2318 and 2415
9 2957, 2349 and 2798
10 2788, 2947, 2740 and 2742
11 2307, 2826, 2318, 2349 and
  2209
12 2307, 2745, 2599, 2597,
  2797, 2957, 2349, 2299 and
  2839
13 2956, 2905 and 2909
14 2798 and 2318
15 2946 and 2307
16 2307, 2745, 2798, 2807,
  2415 and 2299

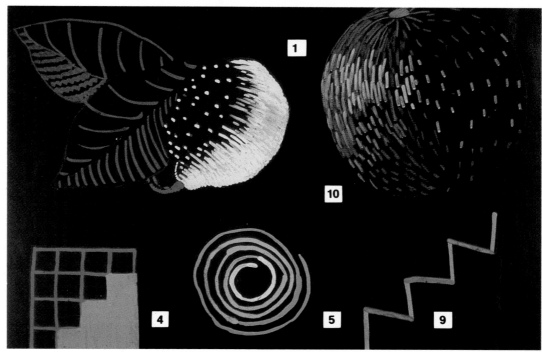

RAFFIA AND FLOWERS

Richelieu work, traditional European embroidery, surfaces in a novel and simplified form in these embroidered mats. Some of the leaves and flowers use rainbow-colored threads, the shaded colors appearing at random.

MATERIALS

Circular or oval woven raffia tablemats

Chenille needle size 24
Glue and spreader

Threads
DMC stranded cotton in the following colors:
yellow 307, 973; **pink** 603, 605, 718; **red** 321, 606, 815; **mauve** 553; **green** 699, 904, 906; **blue** 792, 703, 704; **shaded green** 123, 124; **shaded pink** 116; **shaded yellow** 104; **black** 310

Embroidery Stitches
Buttonhole stitch, long and short stitch, straight stitch.

DIRECTIONS

▨ Trace the designs from the photograph and enlarge them to fit the mats (see page 10). Transfer the design to the mats using the carbon paper method given on page 11.

▨ To prevent the raffia from fraying when the edges are cut, spread a thin film of glue over the narrow areas of the design and the edges of the flowers and leaves, keeping the glue ⅛in (3mm) inside the edges of the design. Leave the mats to dry thoroughly.

▨ Cut away the areas of raffia which are indicated on the design using a sharp pair of scissors.
▨ Use the photograph as a color and stitch guide and work with six strands of thread throughout. Embroider the leaves, joining strips and mat edges in buttonhole stitch and keep the stitches close together to completely cover the raffia beneath.
▨ Edge the flowers in closely worked buttonhole stitch, but with the uprights of the stitches irregularly sized.
▨ Fill in the centers of the flowers with long and short stitch, and pick out the leaf veins with straight stitch.

Trace the design from this guide, then enlarge it to fit the size of your raffia mats (see page 10).

100

NATURE OBSERVED

Sunday in the country, French style, requires an elegantly packed picnic feast, complete with a freshly laundered tablecloth of enormous charm. The cloth is scattered with fruit, nuts, seed heads and insects, the latter so meticulously observed and so lifelike that they might just have jumped on to share the feast. Some 31 colors are used to create this gem of botanical accuracy, but the result is so delightful that it is well worth the attention to detail and the extra effort involved.

Size 77in × 91½in (192cm × 232cm).

MATERIALS

2⅝yd (2.4m) of 80in (200cm) wide fine cream linen or cotton fabric Matching sewing thread	Dressmakers' carbon paper Crewel needle size 6 or 7 Large embroidery hoop

Threads

DMC stranded cotton: one skein each of **brown** 435, 632, 898 and 3064, **green** 367, 471, 472, 734, 3051 and 3053, **yellow** 676, 726 and 3078, **blue** 826, **gold** 783 and 3045, **turquoise** 991, **rust** 918, **tan** 781, **beige** 822 and 3047, **cream** 712, **red** 350 and 498, **gray** 642, **white** and **black**

Embroidery stitches

Satin stitch, long and short stitch and stem stitch.

DIRECTIONS

▦ Trace the motifs, which are shown full size.

▦ Using the photograph as a guide to position, transfer the motifs to the fabric with dressmakers' carbon paper.

▦ Work with the fabric stretched in the embroidery hoop, re-positioning it as necessary. Embroider the motifs mainly in satin stitch and long and short stitch, picking out the details in stem stitch. Use the close-up photograph as a stitch and color blending guide.

▦ Embroider the grasses, bee, small yellow insect and small blue insect using two strands of thread in the needle. Complete the rest of the design using three strands of thread throughout.

▦ When the embroidery is finished, place the fabric face down on a well-padded surface and press it lightly, taking care not to crush the stitches.

▦ Turn under a double ¾in (2cm) hem all around the fabric and hem by hand. Press the hem.

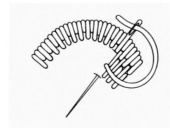

long and short stitch

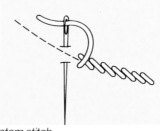

stem stitch

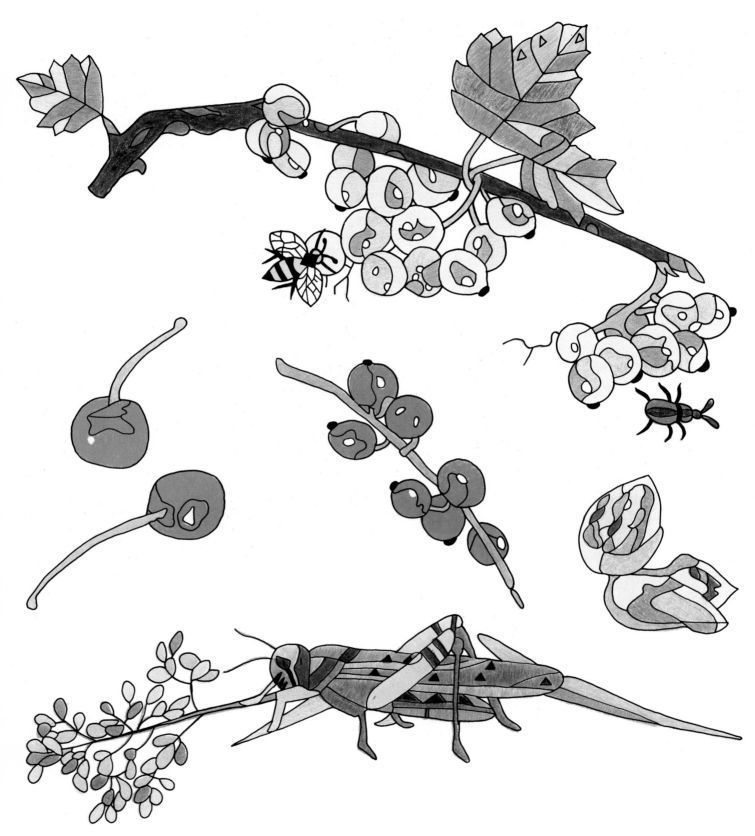

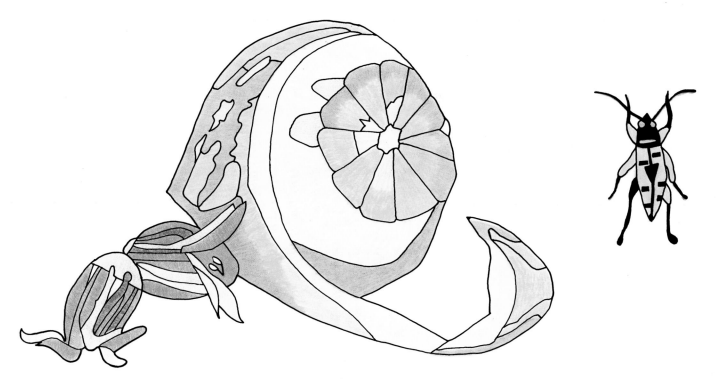

KEY

- 350
- 498
- 918
- 898
- 632
- 435
- 3064
- 781
- 783
- 726
- 676
- 3078
- 3047
- 3045
- 822
- 712
- 3051
- 367
- 471
- 472
- 3053
- 734
- 826
- 991
- 642
- black
- white

HOLIDAY FUN CURTAIN

This bright, cheerful door curtain, an effective screen between a cool interior and the blazing sun outside, is made by threading colorful strips of bias binding through the open mesh of the net. It's so easy that even a child could do it, instantly turning a utilitarian screen into something festive and informal, happily at home with cottage flowers and sunny summer days.

Size: made to fit your door or window space.

MATERIALS

Heavy cotton netting with an open mesh (the holes should be distributed in a regular pattern and large enough to hold the folded tape easily)
1in (2.5cm) wide bias binding in **green, yellow, red, pink, violet,**

blue and **black** (market stalls are often a cheap source)
4in (10cm) wide **white** fringe for lower edge
Bodkin for threading
Matching thread

DIRECTIONS

▦ Measure the door or window opening and cut fabric to this size, adding 4in (10cm) to the width for side hem allowances plus ease, and a sufficient allowance to the length for the desired finish at the top edge.

▦ Turn under a double ⅝in (1.5cm) hem down both side edges; pin, tack and stitch.

▦ Turn up lower edge of curtain to right side for ⅜in (1cm); pin and tack. Position fringe over turned-up edge, turning in the outer edges, in line with side hems. Pin, tack and topstitch fringe in place.

▦ Finish the top edge of the curtain in the desired way.

▦ Using pins, mark the position of the design, about one design width from lower edge. The spacing will depend to some extent on the length of the curtain, but it would be better to have more plain curtain above the design than below.

▦ Thread a manageable length – about 16in (40cm) – of binding through the bodkin, folding the binding in half widthwise, with raw edges inside. Following the diagram for colors and pattern, weave the bodkin in and out through the natural gaps in the fabric. Cut the binding at the end of each line of the design, leaving loose ends of equal length – about ⅜in (1cm) at either end.

Note The curtain can either be finished at the top with ordinary curtain tape (which would then be left ungathered) and hung from a curtain rail or pole, or you could make a casing at the top and thread this over a dowel or pole.

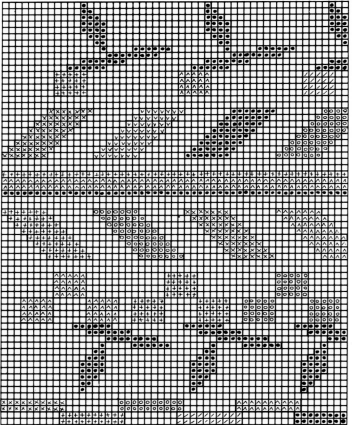

KEY

● Green
○ Yellow
× Red

∧ Pink
∨ Violet
+ Blue
/ Black

CHARACTER NAPKIN

The ultimate refinement for a table set with traditional blue-and-white porcelain ware, this napkin decorated with drawn-threadwork and Chinese characters worked in padded satin stitch will add to the authenticity of any Chinese meal.

Size 16¾in × 16¾in (42cm × 42cm).

MATERIALS

18in × 18in (45cm × 45cm) square of fine white evenweave cotton or linen fabric Crewel needle size 6 or 7	Dressmakers' carbon paper in a dark color Embroidery hoop

Threads
DMC stranded cotton: one skein each of **blue** *798 and* **white**

Embroidery stitches
Padded satin stitch for the motifs and hem stitch for the border.

DIRECTIONS

BORDER EMBROIDERY

▣ Withdraw sufficient threads to make a narrow border around the square of fabric, approximately 1in (2.5cm) from the raw edge. Finish the drawn corners by threading short lengths of the strands back into the fabric.

▣ Turn under ¼in (6mm) and then turn a hem so that the fold is just below the edge of the border. Miter the corners (page 14), and pin and tack the hem in place.

▣ Work a row of hem stitching to secure the hem using three strands of the white thread. Take each stitch around a group of three or four threads, depending on the weight of fabric being used. Repeat the hem stitching at the other side of the border to make a ladder pattern. Press the hem.

hem stitch

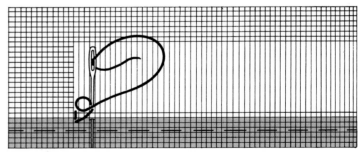

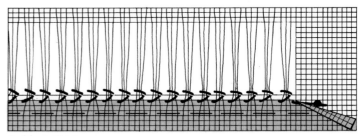

ladder pattern

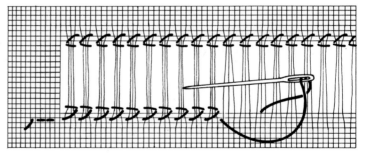

MOTIF EMBROIDERY

▣ Trace the Chinese character motifs. Using the photograph as a guide to position, transfer the motifs to the napkin using the carbon paper method described on page 11. Stretch the napkin in the embroidery hoop.

▣ Begin the embroidery by forming the padding for the satin stitch. Do this by filling the outlined shapes with close lines of back stitch, using two strands of thread in the needle. Work the back stitch down the length of the shapes, rather than across them.

▣ Finish the embroidery by working satin stitch across the lines of back stitch, using four strands of thread. When the embroidery is finished, place the napkin down on a well-padded surface and press it lightly, taking care not to crush the stitches.

MEDITERRANEAN GARLAND

That occasional chair which fills an unused corner can become an appealing conversation piece with just a little thought. A garland of mimosa, poppies, wild roses, carnations, fuchsias, orange blossom and oleander, with its attendant butterfly and ladybirds, twines around the edge of a drop-in chair seat. To give the appearance of an all-over tapestry cover – with none of the hard work – a patterned damask brocade is used, its geometric pattern cleverly offsetting the summer blooms.

MATERIALS

Piece of upholstery-weight fabric. To calculate the amount measure the width of your chair, from side to side and from back to front, and add 2in (5cm) to each measurement. Crewel needle size 5 or 6. Embroidery hoop.

Threads
DMC stranded cotton – 1 skein of each of the following colors: **ecru** and **white**; **pink** 223, 224, 225, 316, 605, 778, 818, 819, 3688, 3689; **green** 320, 367, 471, 502, 503, 504, 912, 3053, 3347, 3348; **red** 325, 350; **coral** 351; **turquoise** 578; **gold** 676; **yellow** 725, 727, 742, 743, 744, 745, 3078; **bronze** 734; **peach** 754, 945, 951; **beige** 739; **blue** 828, 3325; **blue/gray** 927, 928.

Embroidery Stitches
Satin stitch, long and short stitch, seed stitch, stem stitch, padded satin stitch.

DIRECTIONS

▦ Enlarge the design to fit the chair seat (see page 10). Transfer the design to the fabric using the carbon paper method given on page 11, positioning the garland centrally on the fabric.
▦ Work with the fabric in an embroidery hoop, moving the hoop as necessary. Using the photograph and diagram as guides, embroider the flowers and leaves in satin stitch and long and short stitch, and pick out the details at the center of the flowers with seed stitch. Work the stems in stem stitch, and the flower buds and the spray of mimosa in padded satin stitch. Use three strands of thread throughout.
▦ When the embroidery is completed, place it face down on a well-padded surface and press lightly, taking care not to crush the stitches.

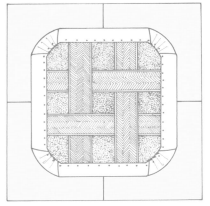
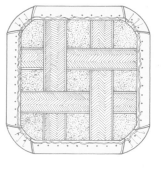
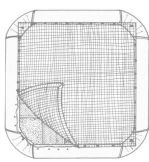

▦ Knock out the seat from the chair. Remove the hessian base and the old top cover from the seat using a ripping chisel and hammer.
▦ Mark center of embroidery on all sides. Place the embroidery wrong side up on a flat surface. Center the chair seat over the embroidery, making sure that the design is facing in the right direction.
▦ Pull the embroidered fabric firmly to the underside of the seat and tack in place, working from the center of each side outwards. Tack each corner in position, smoothing over the fabric to give a rounded effect.
▦ Cut a piece of hessian on the straight of grain the size of the chair seat base. Turn under the raw edges and tack in place all round the seat covering the edges of the embroidered fabric and rounding the corners.

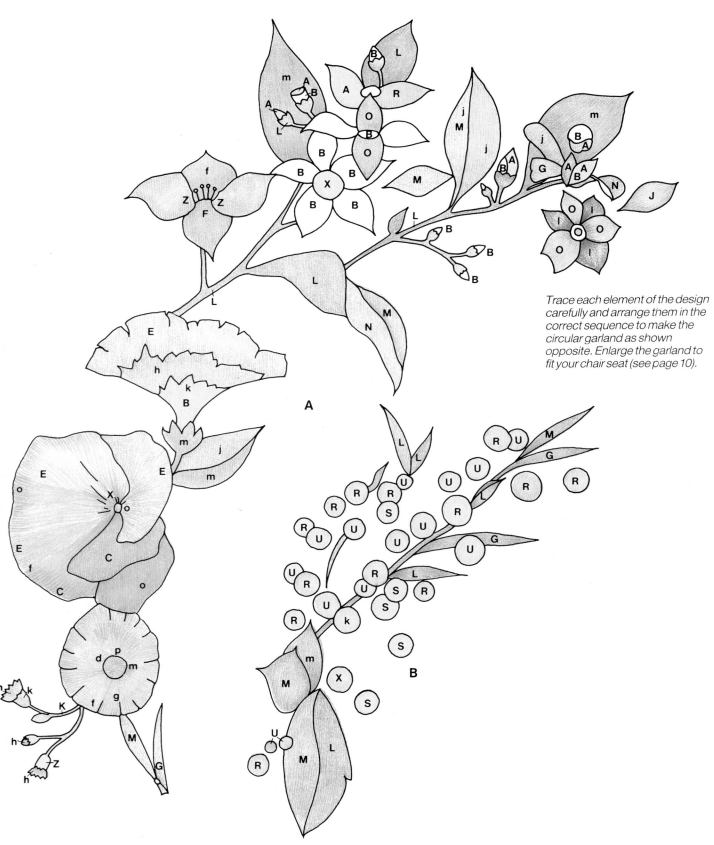

Trace each element of the design carefully and arrange them in the correct sequence to make the circular garland as shown opposite. Enlarge the garland to fit your chair seat (see page 10).

KEY

A	ecru
B	white
C	223
D	224
E	225
F	316
G	320
H	350
I	351
J	367
K	471
L	502
M	503
N	504
O	598
P	605
Q	676
R	725
S	727
T	734
U	742
V	743
W	744
X	745
Y	754
Z	778
a	739
b	818
c	819
d	828
e	912
f	927
g	928
h	945
i	951
j	3055
k	3078
l	3325
m	3347
n	3348
o	3688
p	3689
q	326

FISH FANTASY

A fine collection of fish with their asymmetrical shapes and gorgeous details has been caught and laid out for display – embroider them in hot, tropical colors for cushions as stunning as pictures. Don't labor over the close regularity of the stitches; on a white background the gaps will give you a painterly quality.

MATERIALS

25in (63cm) × 18in (48cm) white cotton fabric	Crewel needle size 6 or 7 Embroidery hoop

Threads
DMC stranded cotton – 1 skein of each of the following:
CUSHION A: **blue** 517, 518, 519, 747; **yellow** 704; **pink** 956; **pale green** 955; **shaded green** 123
CUSHION B: **green** 699, 702, 704; **shaded green** 114; **orange** 970, 972; **yellow** 973; **black** 310
CUSHION C: **green** 699, 701, 890; **blue** 797, 809; **kingfisher** 996; **shaded blue** 113; **yellow** 973; **red** 606; **black** 310

Embroidery Stitches
Long and short stitch, satin stitch, straight stitch.

DIRECTIONS

▦ Enlarge the design to the measurements given on the pattern (see page 10). Transfer the design to the fabric using one of the methods given on page 11 and positioning it as shown in the diagram.
▦ Work with the fabric stretched in an embroidery hoop, moving the hoop as necessary.
▦ Using the close-up photograph as a stitch guide,

embroider the fish in long and short stitch and in satin stitch, and pick out the details in straight stitch. Use three strands of thread throughout.
▦ When the embroidery is completed, place it face down on a well-padded surface and press lightly, taking care not to crush the stitches.
▦ Instructions for making up the cushion covers are on page 15.

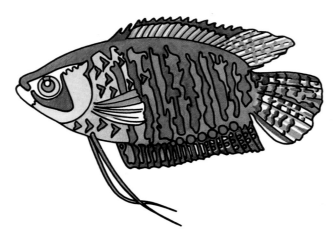

Trace the fish designs from these pictures, which are also guides to the colors used on each fish. The photograph above shows how the embroidery is worked to allow the fabric to show through.

DRAGONFLY BEDLINEN

There is no need to lie awake counting sheep when you could sleep peacefully, dreaming of dragonflies dancing over water. This very delicate set consists of a pillowcase hand embroidered with dragonfly motifs and a machine embroidered and quilted duvet cover, crossed and edged with silver piping, and a pillowcase to match. The cover is of a typically French design, with the center left open so that the duvet can be inserted through it. If you prefer, you could fill the central square and make a conventional opening at the bottom (see page 152).

Sizes Finished duvet cover 80in × 80in (200cm × 200cm) to fit standard double duvet; pillowcases 30in × 22in (75cm × 55cm).

MATERIALS

DRAGONFLY PILLOWCASE

1½yd (1.4m) of 36in (90cm) wide white cotton piqué
3yd (2.7m) of ready-made (washable) silver piping

White sewing thread
Crewel needle size 4 or 5
Dressmakers' carbon paper
Large embroidery hoop

GEOMETRIC PILLOWCASE

1½yd (1.4m) of 36in (90cm) wide white cotton piqué
5½yd (5m) of ready-made

(washable) silver piping
White sewing thread

DUVET COVER

5¾yd (5.2m) of 36in (90cm) wide white cotton piqué
4¾yd (4.2m) of 88in (220cm) wide cotton sheeting for back and inner lining
2yd (2m) of 100in (250cm) wide

medium-weight polyester wadding
30½yd (28m) of ready-made (washable) silver piping
White sewing thread
Light colored pencil

Threads

DRAGONFLY PILLOWCASE

*Two reels of DMC **silver** thread 281*
Anchor coton à broder size 16:

*one skein each of **gray** 398 and 399, and two skeins of **white** 1*

GEOMETRIC PILLOWCASE

*Two reels of DMC **silver** thread 281*

Embroidery stitches

Couching, padded satin stitch; these are used in the Dragonfly pillowcase. The Geometric pillowcase and the Duvet cover are both machine stitched.

DIRECTIONS

DRAGONFLY PILLOWCASE

▨ Cut a piece measuring 32in × 32in (80cm × 60cm) from the fabric. This will be the front of the pillowcase.
▨ Trace the dragonfly design and enlarge it to the required dimensions, as shown on page 10.

▨ Using the photograph as a guide to position, transfer the design to the top left-hand corner of the fabric, using dressmakers' carbon paper and leaving a margin of 1in (2.5cm) from the raw edges.
▨ Working with the fabric stretched in the embroidery hoop, embroider the lines in couched silver thread and the dragonflies in padded satin stitch with the white thread. Embroider the spots in padded satin stitch in a random mixture of silver, white and gray, as seen in the photograph.
▨ When you have finished the embroidery, place the fabric face down on a well-padded surface and press it lightly, taking care not to crush the stitches. Trim the edges so that the finished front section measures 31¼in × 23¼in (78cm × 58cm).

FINISHING THE PILLOWCASE

▨ Cut out a rectangle of fabric 32⅝in × 23¼in (81.5cm × 58cm) for the back and another rectangle 23¼in × 7in (58cm × 17.5cm) for the flap.
▨ Turn under 2in (5cm) to the wrong side along one short edge of the back piece and then turn under ⅜in (1cm) along the raw edge to make a 1⅝in (2in) deep hem. Stitch in place.
▨ Turn under a double 2in (5cm) hem to the wrong side along one long edge of the flap. Pin, tack and stitch in place.
▨ Pin the piping to the right side of the embroidered front. The piping should face inwards to the center all around the edge. Stitch the piping in place ⅝in (1.5cm) from the raw edges.
▨ Assemble the pillowcase by placing the back section on top of the piped front with the right sides of the fabric facing. Align the hemmed edge of the back with the seam line on the front. Place the flap right side down over the hemmed edge of the back, matching the long raw edge of the flap with the raw edge on the front. Pin, tack and stitch, following the line of stitching for the piping.
▨ Trim and finish the raw edges, then turn the pillowcase right side out with the flap on the inside. Press the seams.

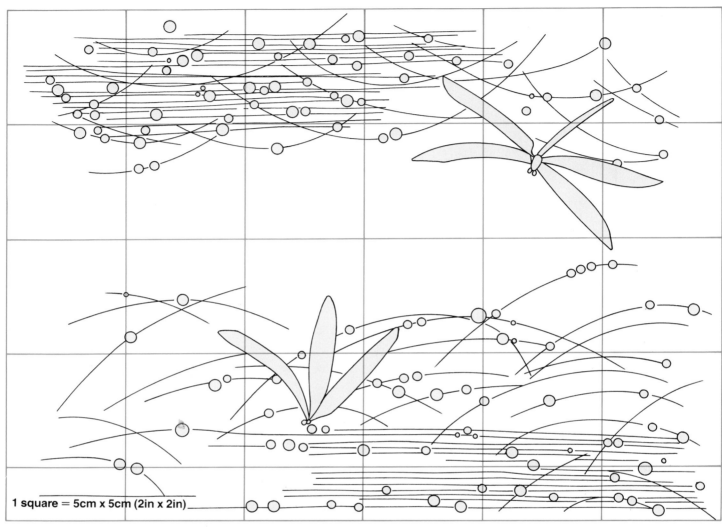

1 square = 5cm x 5cm (2in x 2in)

GEOMETRIC PILLOWCASE

▦ Cut a piece of cotton piqué to measure 25½cm × 17¼in (63cm × 43cm) for the center front.

▦ With silver thread on top and white sewing cotton in the bobbin, stitch the pattern of crossing lines. Use the photograph as a guide, and position the outermost lines 5in (12.5cm) from the raw edges of the fabric.

▦ Pin the piping to the right side of the fabric. It should face towards the center and run all around the edge. Stitch the piping in place ⅝in (1.5cm) from the raw edges.

▦ Cut two strips of fabric measuring 23¼cm × 4¼in (58cm × 10.5cm) and two strips measuring 31¼cm × 4¼in (78cm × 10.5cm). Join the strips into a

frame with mitered darts, starting ⅝in (1.5cm) away from the raw inner edge and tapering to nothing at the outside edge. Trim and press.

▦ Stitch the border frame to the central piece, following the stitching line of the piping and stitching the two long sides first and then the two short ones.

▦ Finish the pillowcase in the same way as the Dragonfly pillowcase.

DUVET COVER

▦ Cut eight rectangles measuring 25¼in × 25¼in (63cm × 63cm) and cut the same from wadding.

▦ Using light colored pencil, draw the seam line on the right side around each fabric piece, ⅝in

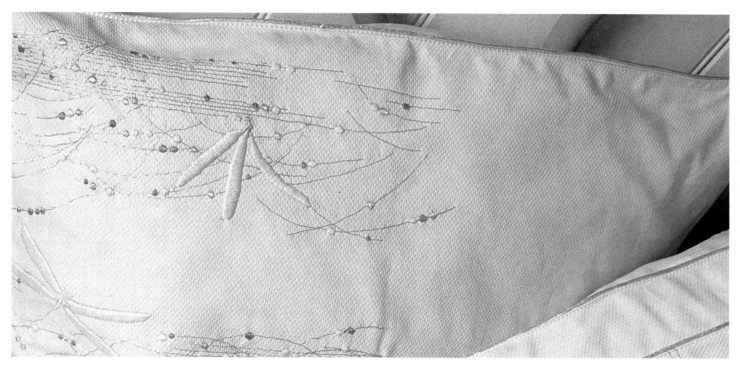

(1.5cm) from the raw edge.

▦ Back each fabric piece with a piece of wadding and tack horizontally and vertically. Using the diagram as a guide, quilt each of the squares with long machine straight stitches and the white sewing thread.

▦ Cut 25¼in (63cm) lengths of piping and stitch one each to the bottom edges of A, B and C and the top edges of F, G and H.

▦ Stitch A, D and F together to make a long strip. Trim wadding back to the seam line and trim ⅜in and ¼in (1cm and 5mm) from the seam allowances of the piping cord at each side of the seams, to layer the seam allowances. Press seams open.

▦ Join C, E and H in the same way. Stitch a length of piping, with the piping lying inwards and raw edges matching, to the inside edge of each long strip.

▦ Following the diagram, join rectangles B and G to the strips to complete the patchwork effect. Topstitch along all seams, except around the center, close to piping.

▦ Pin piping around the outer edge, rounding the corners gently and with the piping facing inwards. Stitch in position.

▦ Cut four strips of piqué and four of wadding, each measuring 81¼in × 7in (203cm × 17.5cm). Pin and tack wadding to the back of each strip, then join the strips, as for the Geometric pillowcase, to make a mitered border frame.

▦ Turn under the seam allowance around the quilted piece and topstitch it to the border, stitching just inside the piping.

▦ Cut two pieces of cotton sheeting the same size as the top. Set one piece aside and pin and stitch the other piece to the top, with right sides together and stitching around the edge of the central opening, following the seam lines of the piping. Cut out the central square from the sheeting and take to the back.

▦ Topstitch around the central opening, close to the piping.

▦ Pin piping around the outer edge, pinning through the top and the backing, with raw edges matching. Stitch in position.

▦ With right sides of duvet top and second piece of sheeting together, stitch around the outer edge, following the line of the piping, and leaving a gap for turning. Turn to the right side and slipstitch to close.

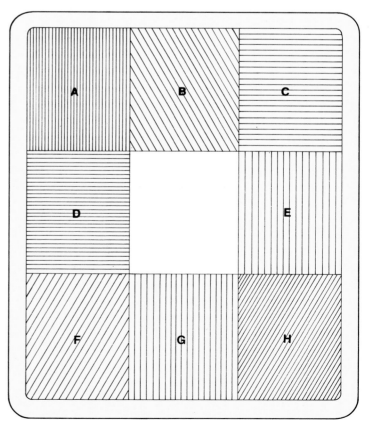

PROVENÇAL PRINTS

These flowered objects were inspired by the traditional fabrics of Provence. Use the violets to decorate a fabric-covered box, a letter file or a jewel case. The tiny swags look particularly fine on a typical abstract French print. Satin stitch and stem stitch in faded colored silks give the fresh-washed, sun-bleached character of the original textile designs.

MATERIALS

SMALL BOX:

Flattish cardboard box with a hinged lid
Cotton fabric with a small geometric design
Crewel needle size 7 or 8
Embroidery hoop

LARGE BOX:

Cardboard box with a lid
Cotton fabric with a large floral design
Cotton fabric with a small geometric design
Crewel needle size 7 or 8
Embroidery hoop

Threads
DMC stranded cotton:
1 skein in each of the following colors:
yellow *677, 745, 746;* **green** *502, 503;* **blue** *930, 931;* **pink** *961;* **black** *310*

Threads: *DMC stranded cotton in colors to match the fabric*

Embroidery Stitches
Long and short stitch, satin stitch, stem stitch.

DIRECTIONS

FOR THE SMALL BOX:
▨ Cut a piece of geometrically patterned fabric to fit the box lid, allowing a margin of 2in (5cm) all round. Enlarge the design to fit across the lid (see page 10).
▨ Transfer the design to the fabric using one of the methods given on page 11.
▨ Work with the fabric stretched in an embroidery hoop, moving the hoop as necessary.
▨ Using the diagram as a color guide, embroider the design in long and short stitch with two strands of thread.

FOR THE LARGE BOX:
▨ Cut a piece of the floral fabric to fit the lid, allowing a margin of 2in (5cm) all round and positioning one or two of the floral sprays attractively on the top of the lid.
▨ Work with the fabric stretched in an embroidery hoop, moving the hoop as necessary.
▨ Using the close-up photograph as a stitch guide, embroider over the flowers and leaves: use long and short stitch for the petals and leaves, pick out tiny areas of color in satin stitch and work the stems and outlines in stem stitch. Use two strands of thread in matching colors throughout.

TO MAKE UP THE BOXES:
▨ Place the embroidery face down on a well-padded surface and press lightly, taking care not to crush the stitches.
▨ Trim the margins to ¾in (2cm) and follow the instructions shown in the diagrams for covering the boxes.

Trace pattern for the small box.

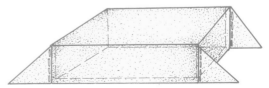

Place the fabric over the box with wrong sides outside. Pin out excess fabric equally at each corner in line with box corners. Remove fabric and stitch each corner level with box edge. Trim off excess fabric and press seam open. Replace over box and stick in place. Fold excess fabric to inside and stick.

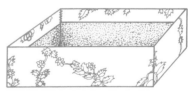

VENETIAN ELEGANCE

Luxuriously elegant cushion covers and a table centerpiece to match make a light-hearted tribute to the great Italian architect of the sixteenth century, Andrea Palladio, who described the classical colonnades which often extended from his villas as 'arms to receive those who come near the house'. These sophisticated embroideries with their gentle, muted tones would blend perfectly with a neutral, modern setting, or with rag-rubbed or marbled walls.

Sizes The cushion covers measure 18½in × 18½in (47cm × 47cm); centerpiece 20in × 20in (50cm × 50cm).

MATERIALS

FOR EACH CUSHION COVER

16in × 16in (40cm × 40cm) of white linen or cotton fabric
Two 20in × 20in (50cm × 50cm) squares of dark fawn linen or cotton fabric
Matching sewing thread

Crewel needle size 5 or 6
Dressmakers' carbon paper in a dark color
Ruler and chalk marking pencil
Large embroidery hoop

CENTERPIECE

20¾in × 20¾in (52cm × 52cm) of white linen or cotton fabric
Matching sewing thread

Crewel needle size 5 or 6
Dressmakers' carbon paper
Large embroidery hoop

Threads

VILLA CAPRA ROTONDA
*DMC stranded cotton: one skein each of **shaded brown** 105, **brown** 433, **beige** 3046 and*
*3047, **gray** 535, 642 and 644, and **ecru***

VILLA GODI
*DMC stranded cotton: one skein each of **shaded brown** 105, **brown** 433, **gray** 415, 535*
*and 646, **blue gray** 927, and **ecru**, and two skeins of **gray** 3072*

VILLA PIOVENE
*DMC stranded cotton: one skein each of **shaded brown** 105, **brown** 407, **gray** 535, **peach***
*950, and **ecru**, and two skeins of **peach** 948*

CENTERPIECE
*DMC stranded cotton: one skein each of **gray** 3072, **blue gray** 926, **blue** 930, **peach** 948,*
***beige** 950, and **fawn** 3046; two skeins of **fawn** 3047, and four skeins of **dark gray** 535*

Embroidery stitches
CUSHION COVERS
Satin stitch for the solid areas and back stitch for the lettering and borders.

CENTERPIECE
Satin stitch and cross stitch for the solid areas and back stitch for the outlines and lettering.

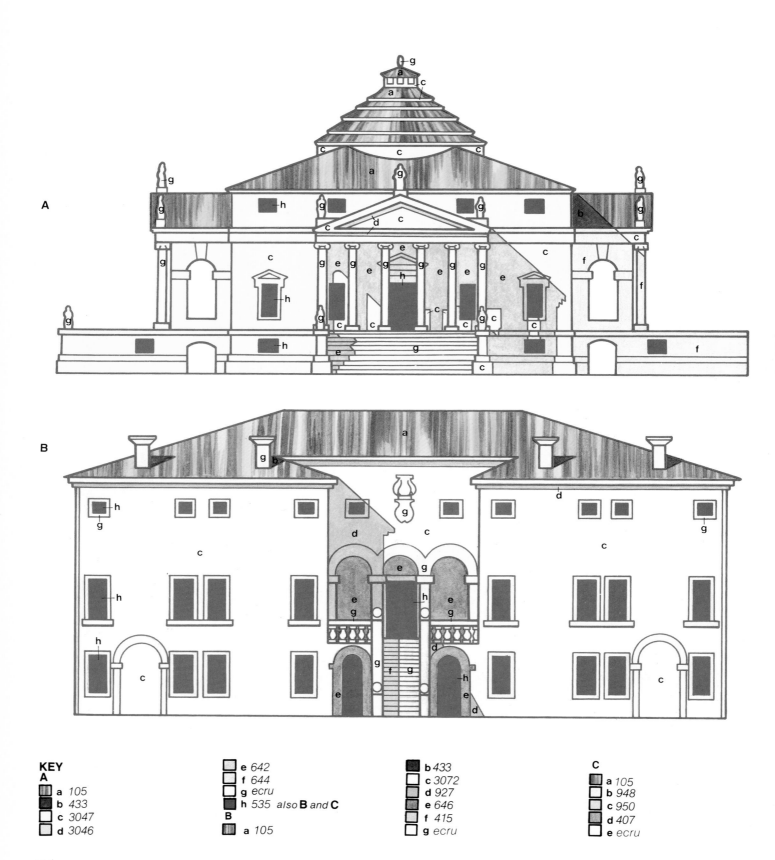

KEY

A

a	*105*
b	*433*
c	*3047*
d	*3046*

e	*642*
f	*644*
g	*ecru*
h	*535 also* **B** *and* **C**

B

a	*105*

b	*433*
c	*3072*
d	*927*
e	*646*
f	*415*
g	*ecru*

C

a	*105*
b	*948*
c	*950*
d	*407*
e	*ecru*

C

DIRECTIONS

CUSHION COVER

▦ Each cushion cover is made in the same way. Start by tracing the chosen design and enlarging it to the required dimensions, as shown on page 10.

▦ Transfer the design to the center of the white fabric using dressmakers' carbon paper. Draw in the border with the chalk pencil and ruler, approximately 2in (5cm) in from the raw edges of the fabric, following the grainlines.

▦ Using the photograph and diagram as stitch guides, embroider the solid areas of the design in satin stitch. Work the border and the appropriate lettering in back stitch using the gray thread, 535. Work with the fabric stretched in the embroidery hoop and use three strands of thread throughout.

▦ When the embroidery is completed, place the fabric face down on a well-padded surface and press it lightly, taking care not to crush the stitches.

FINISHING THE COVER

▦ On one piece of fawn fabric, cut out a central opening measuring 14in (35cm) square to accommodate the embroidered square. Turn under ⅝in (1.5cm) to the wrong side all around the opening, taking care to snip into the corners so that the fabric will lie flat. Tack the turning in place.

▦ Position the fabric over the embroidery so that the embroidery shows evenly through the opening, then pin and tack the layers together. Machine stitch

through the fabric neatly around the opening 2mm (⅛in) from edge.

▦ Pin the front and back pieces of the cushion cover together with right sides facing. Taking a ⅝in (1.5cm) seam allowance, machine stitch them together around the edge.

▦ Trim the corners, press the seam and turn the cover to the right side.

▦ Insert the cushion pad and slipstitch neatly along the opening to close the cover.

ANDREA PALLADIO   1508-1580
VILLA CAPRA ROTONDA
VILLA GODI   VILLA PIOVENE
VILLA ROTONDA

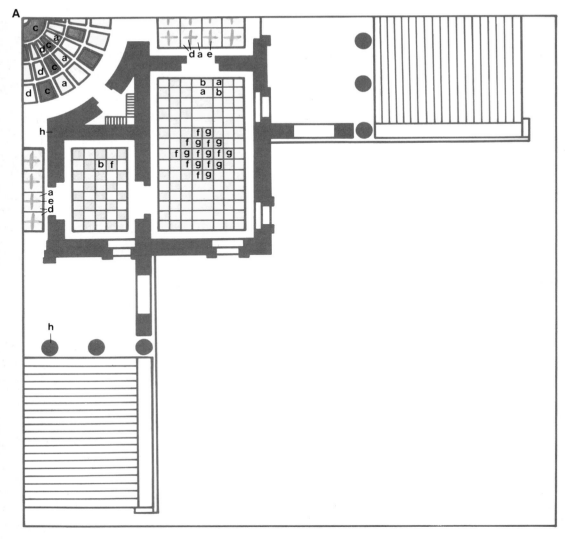

A

CENTERPIECE

🔲 Start by making the border and finishing the edges of the cloth. Turn under and press a ³⁄₈in (1cm) single hem all around the fabric square, mitering the corners neatly. Work a border of close machine zigzag stitch (or satin stitch by hand), covering the raw edges and making the hem.

🔲 Between 3½in and 4in (6.5cm and 8cm) in from the edge of the cloth, make three narrow lines of satin stitch, set close together and running from edge to edge down each side, crossing at the corners.

THE EMBROIDERY

🔲 One quarter of the design is shown, with A being the center point. Trace the complete design

and enlarge it to the required dimensions following the instructions given on page 10.

🔲 Transfer the design to the center of the cloth using the carbon paper method given on page 11.

🔲 Using the photograph as a stitch guide, embroider the solid portions of the design in satin stitch and overstitch them with cross stitch where this is indicated on the design. Work the outlines and lettering in back stitch. Work with the fabric stretched in the embroidery hoop and use the three strands of thread throughout.

🔲 When the embroidery is finished, place the cloth face down on a well-padded surface and

press it lightly, taking care not to crush the stitches.

KEY

☐	**a**	*3047*
☐	**b**	*948*
◼	**c**	*930*
☐	**d**	*3072*
▨	**e**	*926*
☐	**f**	*950*
☐	**g**	*3046*
◼	**h**	*535*

BUTTERFLY PICNIC

A host of butterflies with dazzling wings dances around a damask tablecloth, spilling over onto the napkins – what better setting could you provide for an elegant outdoor feast on a summer's day? Perhaps a few real butterflies will be lured into joining you if you are really lucky. The damask background provides a subtle extra dimension against which you can display as many or as few butterflies as you wish, depending on your personal taste and how energetic you are feeling.

Size: tablecloth 45in×54in (115cm×135cm); napkin 16in×16in (40cm×40cm). The quanties given are for the tablecloth in the photograph but you can easily make yours smaller or larger.

MATERIALS

2¼yd (2m) of 56in (140cm) wide cotton or linen damask – sufficient for one tablecloth and up to six napkins
DMC stranded cotton, one skein each of the following colours: **brown** *300 and 976,* **black** *310,* **gray** *413,* **yellow** *444, 676 and 742,* **orange** *972 and 973,* **blue** *792, 799 and 800,* **turquoise** *995 and 996,* **lilac** *553,* **green** *701, 907, 943, 991 and 993, and* **white**
15½yd (14m) of ½in (13mm) wide blue satin bias binding (for tablecloth and six napkins)
Crewel needle size 6 or 7
Tracing paper
Dressmakers' carbon paper
Matching sewing thread
Note *If the above yarn is unobtainable, refer to page 191.*

DIRECTIONS

▦ Using a pencil mark one rectangle 45in×54in (115cm×135cm) for the tablecloth and six 16in (40cm) squares for the napkins on the damask. Cut out, allowing a small margin of spare fabric around each for fraying.

▦ Enlarge the butterfly motifs onto tracing paper and transfer them to the cloth, using the photograph as a general guide to positioning, but choosing for yourself how many motifs you wish to repeat and where.

▦ Using three strands of thread throughout and keeping the fabric stretched in the embroidery hoop, embroider the motifs. Embroider the butterflies in satin stitch, using the photograph as a stitch guide.

▦ For each napkin, work one or two butterflies in one corner.

▦ When the embroidered pieces are completed, place them face downwards on a well-padded surface and press them lightly.

▦ Trim all pieces back to the marked pencil line. For each napkin, take a 66in (165cm) length of binding. Turn ¼in (6mm) under at one short end and with the binding out flat and matching the folded end to the edge at one side of the napkin, lay the binding along one side, with the edge of the binding a scant ¼in (6mm) in from the raw edge of the napkin. Pin and tack. At the corner adjust the binding so that it will run easily around the corner when brought over to cover the edge. Work around the napkin in this manner. At the final corner, turn under the short raw edge of the binding for ¼in (6mm), folding it at a mitered angle and trimming away any excess length. Make sure that it will completely cover the other end.

▦ Stitch the binding to napkin, bring it over to the wrong side, making mitered folds at the corners, and pin and slipstitch by hand to the other side. (For a more hand-finished effect, machine the binding to the wrong side first and then slipstitch to the right side.)

▦ Complete the tablecloth in the same manner.

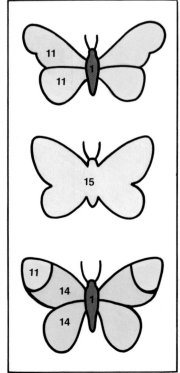

EASTER TABLECLOTH

Breakfast on Easter morning is a family ritual in France as elsewhere, complete with brightly colored eggs, Easter bunnies, lambs and all the other images of springtime and renewal. Here is a tablecloth in the full Easter tradition, dotted with bells, flowers, rabbits seriously engaged in transporting their loads of eggs and hens apparently unperturbed by their multicolored produce. Children will enjoy it openly and adults secretly, and you will inevitably find yourself using it not just for Easter day but for birthday parties and a host of special occasions. These cheerful little designs are immensely versatile and could be used to decorate many other items for children, including pillowcases, pyjamas, T-shirts, bags, or even the hem of a nursery curtain.

Size 49½in × 49½in (124cm × 124cm).

MATERIALS

52in × 52in (130cm × 130cm) of fine white cotton fabric
4¾yd (4.2m) of ⅜in (1cm) wide yellow ribbon

Yellow and white sewing threads
Crewel needle size 5 or 6
Dressmakers' carbon paper
Large embroidery hoop

Threads

DMC stranded cotton: one skein of **yellow** 742 for the chicks; one skein of **blue** 995 for the ribbons; one skein of **brown** 921 for the rabbits; odds and ends stranded cotton in various shades of **green, blue, orange, yellow, beige, ecru, red, pink, mauve, gray, brown** and **black**

Embroidery stitches

Satin stitch, long and short stitch, straight stitch, back stitch and stem stitch.

134

DIRECTIONS

▦ The two motifs shown above and those on page 134 are all shown full size. All other motifs are shown two-thirds full size.

▦ Trace all motifs, then take the small size ones and enlarge them to full size as described on page 10 (in this case the small grid should have ⅜in/1cm squares and the full-size grid should have ⅝in/ 1.5in squares). It may be easier simply to trace over the main outlines of the more complicated motifs and fill in the minor details by hand afterwards. Using the photograph as a guide to position, transfer the motifs to the fabric by . the carbon paper method.

▦ Work with the fabric stretched in the embroidery hoop and re-position it as necessary. Embroider the motifs mainly in satin stitch and long and short stitch, picking out the details in stem stitch, back stitch and straight stitch. Use the close-up photographs as stitch and color blending guides and work with

three strands of thread throughout.

▦ When the embroidery is completed, place the fabric face down on a well-padded surface and press it lightly, taking care not to crush the stitches.

FINISHING

▦ Turn under a double ⅝in (1.5cm) hem along all edges of the fabric, mitering the corners (see page 14). Pin and hem by hand.

▦ Cut the ribbon into four strips of equal length. Join the strips into a square, placing them right sides together and stitching the ends at a 45 degree angle to make mitered corners. Trim and press. Pin the ribbon square in place on the tablecloth, making sure that it is positioned an equal distance from the edge on all sides.

▦ Sew the ribbon to the tablecloth by machine, using either close zigzag stitches or a small running stitches, and keeping close to each edge of the ribbon. Stitch each edge in the same direction, to avoid ruckles.

COUNTRYSIDE DREAMS

Delicate wild roses transform white linen or cotton sheeting into luxurious bedding. One spray looks romantic – several scattered across the fabric cover are a display of consummate skill. The rambling motif looks just as fitting stitched on long curtains of lawn or cotton, which filter the light.

MATERIALS

White cotton sheet, either single- or double-bed size.	*Crewel needle size 7 or 8* *Embroidery hoop*

Threads
Susan Bates Anchor stranded cotton in the following colors: **red** *22, 334;* **pink** *49, 52, 57;* **yellow** *293;* **gold** *306, 307;* **green** *213, 214, 216, 256, 258, 267, 855;* **brown** *905;* **beige** *378;* **cream** *386;* **black** *403;* **white** *1.*

Embroidery Stitches
Stem stitch, padded satin stitch, satin stitch, straight stitch, darning stitch.

DIRECTIONS

▦ Enlarge the design to four times the size of the photograph pattern (see page 10). Transfer the design to the sheet using the pricking and pouncing method given on page 11.

▦ Work with the fabric stretched in an embroidery hoop, moving the hoop as necessary.

▦ Use the photographs as color guides and work with two strands of thread.

▦ Embroider the leaves, stems and rosebuds in closely worked rows of stem stitch to fill each shape.

▦ Embroider the rosehips in padded satin stitch using two shades of red. Work the centers of the roses in satin stitch and pick out the details in straight stitch.

▦ Embroider the rose petals in parallel rows of darning stitch – each stitch should be about ¼in (5mm) long and pick up only one or two threads of fabric.

▦ Work the larger thorns in stem stitch, the smaller ones in straight stitch.

▦ When the embroidery is completed, place it face down on a well-padded surface and press lightly, taking care not to crush the stitches.

Embroider a section of the spray on a pillowcase to complement the bedcover. Place the motif at the sides of the pillowcase, rather than in the center, to avoid sleeping on the embroidery.

Trace off the design and enlarge it (see page 10) so that it is approximately four times larger than the tracing. Transfer it to the sheet using the pricking and pouncing method given on page 11. Use the photograph as a guide to the stitching and the colors. When working the rose petals, keep the stitches of equal size.

CULINARY ALLUSIONS

Whether your cuisine is enriched with fresh herbs snipped from your garden or a savory mixture of seafoods, these attractive aprons should help to make cooking a pleasure rather than a chore. The marine collection is embroidered entirely in stem stitch against a blue background, while the chives and parsley, complete with realistic-looking scissors and string, are embroidered in a variety of stitches. Both aprons are made to the same basic pattern, though the herbal version has patch pockets.

Size 32in × 32in (80cm × 80cm).

MATERIALS

SEAFOOD APRON
1yd (1m) of 36in (90cm) wide blue cotton fabric
Matching sewing thread
3yd (2.9m) of ¾in (2cm) wide matching blue tape

Dressmakers' pattern paper
Dressmakers' carbon paper in a light color
Crewel needle size 3 or 4
Large embroidery hoop

HERB APRON
1¼yd (1.1m) of 36in (90cm) wide white cotton fabric
Matching sewing thread
3yd (2.9m) of ¾in (2cm) wide white tape
Dressmakers' pattern paper

Dressmakers' carbon paper
Dressmakers' chalk pencil
Crewel needles size 6 and 7
Large chenille needle
Large embroidery hoop

Threads
SEAFOOD APRON
*DMC stranded cotton: four skeins of **white***

HERB APRON
*DMC stranded cotton: one skein each of **ecru**, **beige** 640 and 3047, **gray** 318, 414, 415 and*
*762, and two skeins each of **green** 122 and 988*

Embroidery stitches
SEAFOOD APRON
Stem stitch

HERB APRON
Stem stitch, straight stitch, long and short stitch and Chinese knots.

DIRECTIONS

MAKING THE APRON
▦ Scale up the diagram on dressmakers' pattern paper and cut out. For the seafood apron, cut out the main piece and a matching pair of facings; for the herb apron, cut out the main piece, a pair of facings and two patch pockets.
▦ Taking a ⅜in (1cm) seam

allowance and with right sides together, stitch a facing to each side of the apron, from neck edge to side edge. Holding facings out flat, make a narrow hem on all other edges, including short edges of facings. Turn under and press a ⅜in (1cm) seam along remaining long edge of each facing. Bring the facings to the underside of the apron and press.

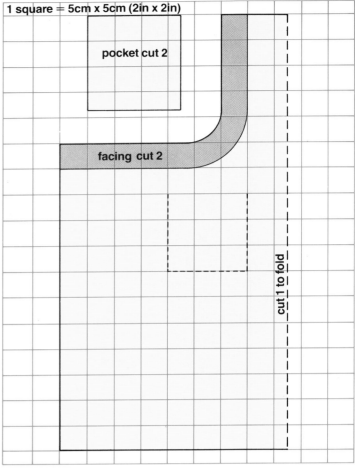

1 square = 5cm x 5cm (2in x 2in)

pocket cut 2

facing cut 2

cut 1 to fold

Topstitch facings to apron, close to both pressed edges, leaving a casing for the tape.

Cut the tape into two equal lengths and thread through the casing. Adjust to leave an adequate length for ties at neck and back, then stitch across at neck edge and side to hold ties in position.

For herb apron, turn under ⅜in (1cm) and then 1in (2.5cm) along the top edge of each pocket section and stitch. Press under a double hem of ⅜in (1cm) on all other sides of each pocket and topstitch in place on apron.

SEAFOOD EMBROIDERY

Trace the fish and shell design and enlarge it to the dimensions given, as shown on page 10.

Following the photograph as a guide to position, transfer the individual motifs to the apron, using dressmakers' carbon paper.

Working with the apron stretched in an embroidery hoop, embroider the motifs in stem stitch, using the stranded cotton double in the needle.

When the embroidery is finished, place the apron face down on a well-padded surface and press it lightly, taking care not to crush the stitches.

HERB EMBROIDERY

Scale up the chive and parsley motifs and, using the photograph as a guide to position, transfer them to the apron with dressmakers' carbon paper.

Slip a pair of scissors into the other pocket and draw around the outline of the handles, using the dressmakers' chalk pencil. On the front of the same pocket, draw a line to represent the piece of string.

Working with the apron stretched in an embroidery hoop, embroider the motifs as follows: the chives and parsley stems are worked in stem stitch, using two strands of green and the size 7 crewel needle.

The bobbles on the parsley are formed by Chinese knots worked with six strands of green 988 and 12 strands of green 122 together in the chenille needle. They are linked to the parsley stems with

1 square = 2.5cm x 2.5cm (1in x 1in)

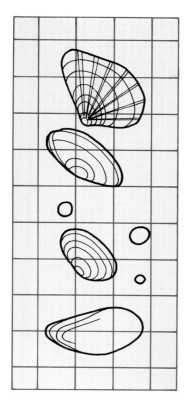

straight stitches, worked with two strands of the same green as the relevant stem and using the size 7 needle.

▦ Embroider the string in stem stitch, using six strands each of ecru, beige 640 and beige 3047 together in the chenille needle.

▦ The scissors are embroidered in long and short stitch in the four shades of gray. Use three strands of thread in the size 6 crewel needle and blend the colors from light to dark to achieve the effect of light shining at an angle on the scissors.

LEMON AND LIME SQUARES

Cross stitch is easy to follow and satisfyingly simple to do well, but you need not limit yourself to squared canvas if you enjoy this embroidery. The lemons and leaves are stitched through canvas which provides an easy-to-use grid on a fine-weave white, ready-made tablecloth. The lime and leaf-green cross-stitched overcloth is made by joining embroidered squares with herringbone stitches. There's a variety of designs, offering you all kinds of different settings.

MATERIALS FOR TABLECLOTH

Ready-made white cotton or linen tablecloth, approximately 6ft (1.8m) × 6ft 6in (2m)

8 pieces of single-thread 12-gauge canvas, each 6in (15cm) × 7in (18cm)
Crewel needle size 5 or 6

Threads
DMC stranded cotton in the following colors:
*6 skeins of **green** 701, 895; 5 skeins of **yellow** 445; 4 skeins of **yellow** 444, 972; 3 skeins of **green** 987; 3 skeins of **cream** 746*

Embroidery Stitch
Cross stitch: each square on the chart represents one cross stitch worked over one vertical and one horizontal canvas thread.

DIRECTIONS FOR TABLECLOTH

▦ Each piece of canvas is slightly larger than the lemon motif, providing a regular grid on which to work the cross-stitch lemons.
▦ Tack the rectangles of canvas to the tablecloth, positioning them as shown in the photograph with two lemon motifs at each corner of the cloth.
▦ Embroider the design carefully following the chart. Stitch base cloth, using six strands of thread.
▦ When the embroidery is completed, carefully cut away the surplus canvas close to the stitching. Gently pull out the remaining canvas threads from beneath the stitching with a pair of tweezers: avoid snagging.
▦ Place the cloth face down on a well-padded surface and press lightly, taking care not to crush the stitches.

Place the motifs at each corner.

MATERIALS FOR OVERCLOTH

*6 squares of white even-weave
12-gauge fabric, each 14in
(35cm) × 14in (35cm)*

*Crewel needle size 7 or 8
Crewel needle size 4 or 5
White sewing thread*

Threads
*DMC stranded cotton: 4 skeins of
each of the following colors:
design 1 **green** 989, 3348;
design 2 **green** 580, 909; design
3 **green** 3348, **kingfisher blue**
996; design 4 **green** 986, 988;
design 5 **green** 701, 704; design
6 **green** 701, 895; plus 4 skeins
of **green** 701 for joining the
squares*

Embroidery Stitches
*Cross stitch for working the
designs: one square on the chart
represents one cross stitch
worked over one woven block of
the fabric; feather stitch for joining
the squares.*

DIRECTIONS

▦ Run a vertical and a horizontal
line of guide basting through the
center of each square of fabric to
correspond with the center lines
on the charts.

▦ Embroider the designs from
the charts, working from the
center outwards. Use three
strands of thread and the finer
crewel needle throughout.

▦ Repeat the patterns on the
charts until each area of
embroidery measures 12in
(30cm) × 12in (30cm).

▦ Turn a double ⅜in (1cm) hem
all round each square (see page
14 for instructions for mitering the
corners) and hand stitch with
white thread.

▦ When the squares are
completed, place them face
down on a well-padded surface
and press lightly, taking care not
to crush the stitches.

▦ Join the squares edge to
edge, as shown in the diagram,
by working a row of feather stitch
with six strands of green 701
thread and the larger crewel
needle. Press the joinings lightly.

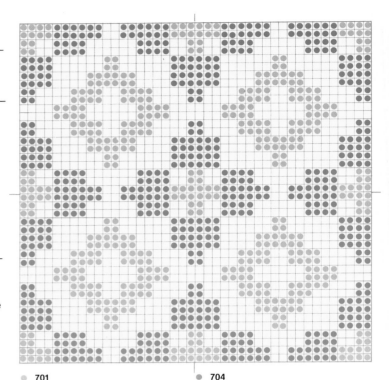

● 701   ● 704

*The overcloth is made up of these
six different cross-stitch squares.*

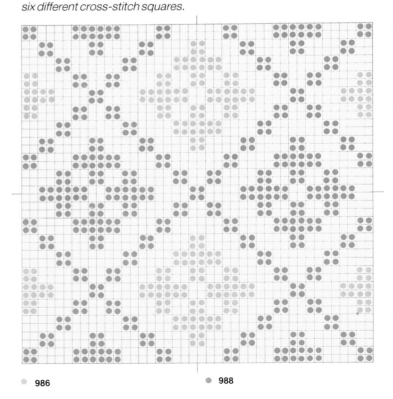

● 986   ● 988

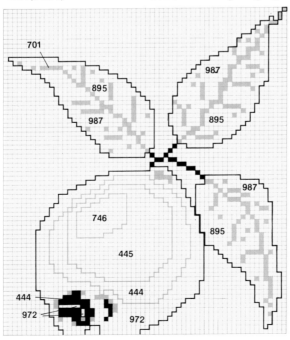

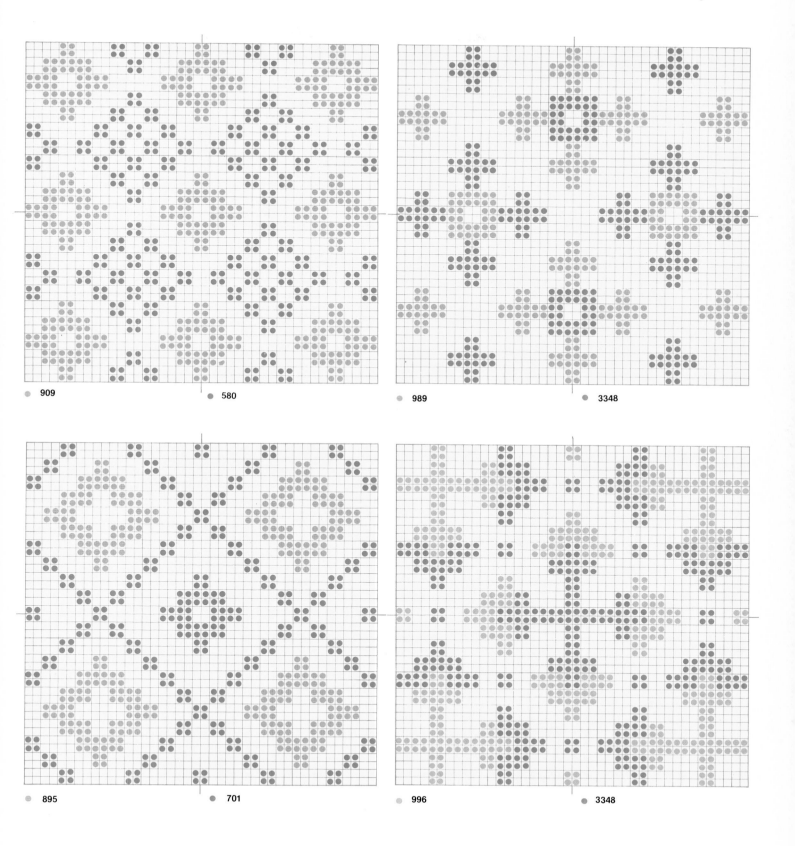

909   580

989   3348

895   701

996   3348

BOUND WITH BOWS

An attractive tablemat and matching napkin help to set the scene for a celebration, giving your table an appropriately light and festive air, whatever the occasion. Choose bright red or green for Christmas or pretty pastels for a summer tea party; pick a contrast fabric which will harmonize with curtains or other elements of your decor, or make a harlequin set with a different color for every member of the family.

Sizes: tablemat approximately 19½in × 11½in (49cm × 29cm); napkin 15¼in (38cm) square.

MATERIALS

Quantities are for one mat and one napkin:	Bonding fabric
⅝yd (50cm) of 36in (90cm) wide plain white cotton	Tracing paper
	Dressmakers' pattern paper
8in (20cm) of 36in (90cm) wide contrast fabric	Matching embroidery cotton
	Matching thread

DIRECTIONS

FOR THE TABLEMAT

▦ Cut a piece of squared paper 20in × 12in (50cm × 30cm). Fold it carefully in half both ways (into four) and press folds. Draw up the diagram onto one side of the folded paper, with the straight edges running along the folded paper edges. Keeping the paper folded, cut along the shaped outer edge. Unfold the pattern.

▦ Using the pattern, cut out one placemat from white cotton – a seam allowance of ¼in (6mm) all around is included.

▦ Now draw in the border on the pattern, making it 1½in (3.5cm) wide all around (this includes seam allowances). Using tracing paper, make patterns for the border – one for the sides and one for the top and bottom, angling the corners so that the strips will join at a mitered angle and adding ¼in (6mm) seam allowances at ends.

▦ Cut two sides and two top/bottom strips from contrast fabric and join to make a continuous border frame. Turn in and tack a ¼in (6mm) allowance around the inner edge, clipping up to the fold where necessary.

▦ With right side of border to wrong side of mat, pin, tack and stitch border to mat, taking a ¼in (6mm) seam allowance all around. Taking notches out of seam allowance where necessary, bring border to right side of mat. Topstitch by machine or blanket stitch by hand to hold border in place around inner edge.

▦ Scale up and trace off bow pattern, once with and once without ribbon ends. Mark both shapes on bonding fabric and cut out roughly, allowing a little extra all around. Iron bonding to wrong side of contrast fabric and cut out both shapes.

▦ Pull back from bow with ends and position at top right corner of mat. Press in place, then blanket stitch around the outer edge and the knot, anchoring the bow. Add crease lines in stem stitch and scattered dots in satin stitch.

▦ Remove backing from bow without ends and iron to wrong side of contrast fabric, then cut out. Blanket stitch around inner lines and knot of contrast bow, adding crease lines in stem stitch as before. Position prepared bow upside down at left-hand corner. Blanket stitch in place, sewing all around the outer edge but only attaching the bow to the mat at either end, leaving the central portion free, to hold the napkin.

FOR THE NAPKIN

▦ Cut out one piece of white cotton 15¼in (38cm) square. Bind the napkin in the same way as the place mat, but cutting strips ⅞in (2.2cm) wide, to make a finished border ⅜in (1cm) wide.

▦ Trace a bow shape and cut from contrast fabric. Iron to bonding fabric, remove backing, and then iron and blanket stitch to napkin, adding stem stitch and satin stitch details as before.

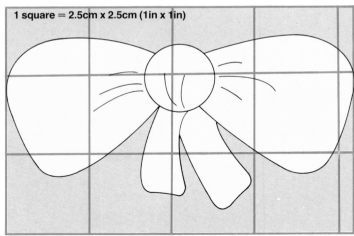

1 square = 2.5cm x 2.5cm (1in x 1in)

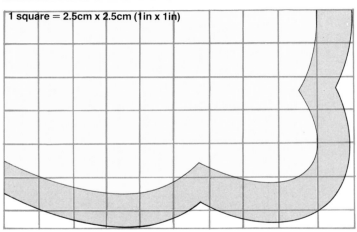

1 square = 2.5cm x 2.5cm (1in x 1in)

HUNGARIAN DUVET COVER

Hungarian folk art captures the profusion and rich colors of tender wild flowers in vivid embroideries that hum with life like a gypsy dance. Here, a collection of the flower motifs that are traditionally used to decorate Magyar blouses are entwined to make a deeper inner border for a glowing duvet cover. The result is splendid, but the cover is not as complicated to embroider as it might appear: the stitches used are basically very simple and the lavish effect comes from the well-planned use of colors.

Size Finished cover emasures 54in × 80in, to fit standard single bed duvet.

MATERIALS

4¾yd (4.2m) of 56in (140cm) wide white cotton sheeting fabric
White sewing thread
1yd (1m) of nylon snap tape

Dressmakers' carbon paper in a dark color
Crewel needle size 3 or 4
Large embroidery hoop
White dress marking chalk

Threads
DMC pearl cotton No. 5: three skeins each of **pink** 335 and 818, **shaded pink** 48, **green** 581, 895 and 993, **shaded green** 92, 101 and 122, **white, shaded brown** 105, and **shaded turquoise** 91, and four skeins each of **red**

666 and 814, **shaded red** 57, 99, 107 and 115, **orange** 900, 817 and 947, **shaded orange** 51, **yellow** 402, 973, and 977, **shaded yellow** 108 and 111, and **shaded blue** 67, 93 and 121

Embroidery stitches
Satin stitch and stem stitch

DIRECTIONS

THE EMBROIDERY
▦ First cut the fabric into two equal rectangles and set one aside for the back of the cover.
▦ Trace the three sections of the garland design and join them carefully into one continuous strip. Enlarge the design to the required dimensions, as shown on page 10, again using tracing paper so that you can reverse it.
▦ Using the diagram as a guide to position, transfer the garland sections to the fabric.
▦ Working with the fabric stretched in the embroidery hoop, embroider the flowers and foliage in satin stitch and the stems in stem stitch.
▦ When the embroidery is completed, place the fabric face down on a well-padded surface and press it lightly, taking care not to crush the stitches.

FINISHING THE COVER
▦ Fold under and stitch a double 1in (2.5cm) hem along the bottom edge of front and back pieces.
▦ Place the front and back together, with right sides facing, aligning the hemmed edges. Sewing along the hemline, machine stitch the two pieces together for 10in (25cm) from each side, leaving a central opening.
▦ Trim the snap tape to measure 1¼in (3cm) longer than the opening. Position the two strips of tape along the edges of the opening so that they will match when the cover is turned to the right side. Stitch along the top and bottom edges of each strip, sewing through the hemmed edge only. Stitch the hems together at each side of the opening, enclosing the raw ends of the tape.
▦ Fold the cover with wrong sides facing and make a French seam around the remaining three sides: pin and stitch ⅜in (1cm) from the edge along all three sides and trim back to ¼in (6mm). Turn the cover wrong side out and stitch along all three sides again, ⅜in (1cm) from the edge, enclosing the raw edges and completing the seam.
▦ Turn the finished cover to the right side and press the seams.

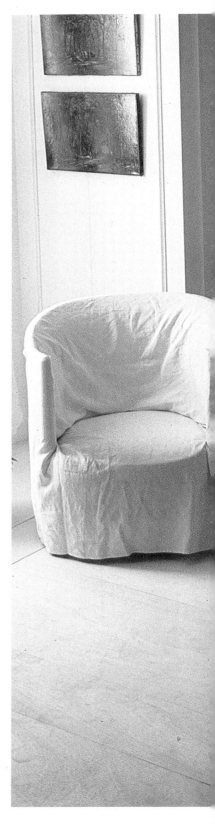

1 *Enlarge to make joined garland 20½in (74cm)*

It will help you to transfer the design if you first rule a base line on the fabric, using tailor's chalk. The line should be 29½in (74cm) long and positioned 24in (60cm) up from the bottom edge of the fabric, and an equal distance in from the sides. Using a set square, rule lines running upwards from each end of the base line, to act as guidelines for the side edges of the garland. The garland runs from **A** (left) to **B** (right) along the bottom line. The sides start with **C** at the bottom left and **A** at the bottom right, and finish with **B** at the top. The tracing is then turned over and repeated at the top, wrong side uppermost, to run from **B** at the

top left to **A** at the top right, flower **A** being repeated at the top left to fill the gap between the two pattern repeats. When stitching the design, blend the colors to achieve a natural effect, varying them as indicated. For the flowers marked **1, 2, 3, 4, 5, 7** and **8**, use colors 115, 48, 57, 335, 107, 666, 818, 814, 900 and 99; flowers marked **6** and **10** are embroidered in colors 973, 977, 108, 402, 111, 817, 947, 51 and 105, and flowers marked **2** and **5** can also be stitched in these colors; for **11** and **12** use 67, 91, 93, 121 and white; and for **9** (stalks and leaves) use 92, 101, 122, 581, 895 and 993.

FALL OF LEAVES

A delicate shadow-work tablecloth of fine organdy, with napkins to match, captures the autumnal splendor of a French forest of sweet chestnut trees at that transitional time of year when the leaves begin to drift earthwards and the nuts ripen to form a delicious harvest to savor through the winter. In this embroidery technique, worked here with the traditional closed herringbone stitch, the threads are carried across the reverse side of a semi-transparent fabric. As shown below, the stitches can be worked from either side of the fabric, and they are used here to convey the impression of sunlight filtering through branches.

Size The tablecloth measures 42in × 77in (107cm × 192cm); each napkin measures 16in × 16in (40cm × 40cm).

MATERIALS

45in (115cm) wide fine cotton organdy as follows: 2½yd (2m) for the cloth 17½in × 17½in (44cm × 44cm) for each napkin	Matching sewing thread Crewel needle size 8 or 9 HB lead pencil Large embroidery hoop

Threads
DMC stranded cotton: one skein each of **brown** 355, 632, 780, **rust** 922 and 976, **gold** 729, and **green** 469, 470, 3051 and 3348

Embroidery stitches
Closed herringbone stitch worked on the reverse of the fabric

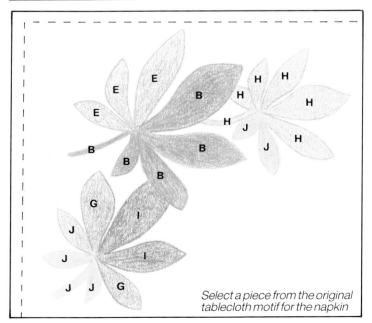

Select a piece from the original tablecloth motif for the napkin

DIRECTIONS

▣ Trace the leaf design and enlarge it to the required dimensions, as shown on page 10.
▣ Using the photograph as a guide to position, transfer the design to the fabric by placing the design under the fabric and tracing it through with the HB pencil. The pencil lines should be on the wrong side of the fabric.
▣ Work with the fabric stretched in the embroidery hoop and reposition it as necessary. With fine fabric of this type it is best to bind your embroidery hoop to help to prevent any possible damage. Take a length of bias binding tape and wrap it firmly round the inner ring of the hoop until all the wood is covered. Secure the ends with masking tape. As a further precaution, and to prevent the fabric from moving in the hoop, place a sheet of tissue paper over the fabric before fitting it in the hoop, then tear away the center, revealing the area to be embroidered.
▣ Embroider the leaves on the reverse side of the fabric in closed herringbone stitch, using two strands of thread in the needle throughout.

closed herringbone stitch right side

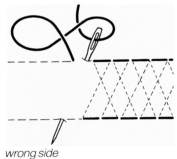

wrong side

▦ When the embroidery is finished, place the fabric face down on a well-padded surface and press it lightly, taking care not to crush the stitches.

▦ Turn under a double ¾in (2cm) hem all around the fabric and hem by hand or machine.

▦ For the napkin, stitch the embroidery in the same way as for the cloth, but use the small leaf design. To finish the napkin, turn under a double ⅜in (1cm) hem and finish as for the cloth.

KEY

A *355*
B *632*
C *780*
D *922*
E *976*
F *729*
G *469*
H *470*
I *3051*
J *3348*

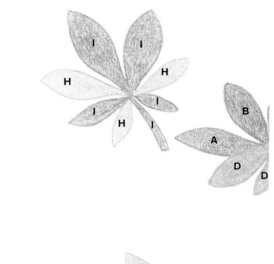

Enlarge 3 times

CELEBRATION TIME

Clouds of net, as light and airy as champagne bubbles and decorated with feathers, ribbons and tiny balls, create a magical party scene for Christmas, a birthday, an engagement, a wedding anniversary or whatever you choose. If you are too inhibited even to dine by candlelight, this is not for you, but if you share the Gallic love for the dramatic and for creating a romantic or festive atmosphere, then you will appreciate this instant transformation.

Sizes: to fit your own requirements.

MATERIALS

FOR THE DOOR CURTAIN

Net fabric – see below for
  quantity
Small amounts of plain cotton
  fabric for appliqué
Chenille braid

¾in (2cm) diameter polystyrene
  balls
Fabric adhesive
Bodkin
Matching thread

FOR THE LAMPSHADE COVER

Net fabric – see below for
  quantity
Chenille braid
¾in (2cm) diameter polystyrene

balls
Fabric adhesive
Matching thread

FOR THE CLOTH

Net fabric – see below for
  quantity
Chenille braid

Feathers
Fabric adhesive
Matching thread

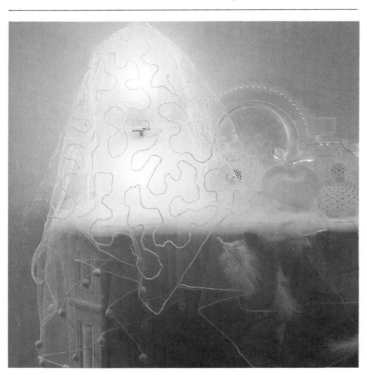

DIRECTIONS

THE DOOR CURTAIN

▦ Measure the door and cut a length of net fabric to this size, plus 1in (2cm) on the width and 3in (7cm) on the length, for top casing and hems.

▦ Turn under a double ¼in (6mm) wide hem on side and base edges of curtain, making neat base corners. Pin, tack and stitch hems in place.

▦ At the top edge, turn under a double 1¼in (3mm) wide hem to form a casing; pin, tack and stitch in place along the lower folded edge.

▦ Using fabric adhesive, fix braid haphazardly over the curtain in a loopy design, adding polystyrene balls. Push a hole straight through the center of each ball with a bodkin and push in the folded braid, till the end just comes through on the opposite side.

▦ Add appliqué shapes: decide on a simple flower and leaf design and mark the shapes onto the fabric. Stitch round each shape just inside the outline. Cut out each shape. Pin appliqué shapes onto the curtain, set your sewing-machine to a close zigzag stitch and work around each shape. Add trails of braid for stamens.

▦ Thread on covered wire and hang above the door.

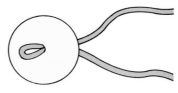

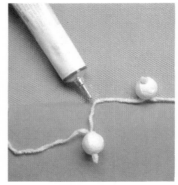

THE LAMPSHADE

▦ Measure from the center of the top of the existing lampshade to the desired length of the cover and cut out a square to twice this length.

▦ Turn up a tiny hem to the right side and handstitch in place with small stitches. With edge of braid butting the outer edge of net, glue braid over edge of cover, adding polystyrene balls at intervals, as for the door curtain.

▦ Cut a 2in (5cm) diameter hole

setting the scene

from the center of the square.
Finish the edge by adding braid in
the same way as the hem edge.
▦ Add random patterns of braid
all over the square.
▦ Place the net cover over the
existing lampshade. Make sure
that your lampshade will keep the
net at a safe distance from the
light bulb, so that there is no
danger that it might catch fire,
and use a low wattage bulb.
Never try to cover a live flame,
even if the distance between the

flame and the net seems safe.

THE CLOTH
▦ Cut a square of fabric to the
desired size and finish the outer
edge as for the lampshade.
▦ Work tiny bars in the cloth at
positions chosen for the feathers.
Slot the feathers through the bars
to hold them in place (in this way
they can easily be removed when
you need to wash the cloth).

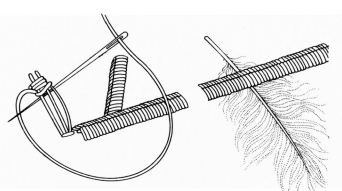

DAMASK DELIGHT

Sprays of pink and creamy flowers and grasses – unashamedly feminine and romantic – are set against a slightly unusual background of checkered pink damask, creating a feeling of elegance and great charm. The resulting tablecloth would look equally at home in a formal dining room, perhaps complemented by bowls of fresh flowers, or spread over a garden table. A matching cloth of striped pink and white cotton underneath protects the carefully embroidered damask and could be used to give it greater coverage.

Size 77½cm × 77½cm (194cm × 194cm).

MATERIALS

80cm × 80cm (200cm × 200cm) of pink-and-white checkered damask fabric
Matching thread

Dressmakers' carbon paper
Crewel needle size 4 or 5
Large embroidery hoop

Threads
DMC stranded cotton: one skein each of **gray** 415 and 452, **green** 368 and 3051, **pink** 335, 776, 778 and 819, and **blue gray** 927; two skeins each of **gray** 3024, **green** 3053, **pink** 223 and 3354, and **dull gold** 3032, and three skeins each of **green** 369, **gray** 642, and **beige** 822

Embroidery stitches
Long and short stitch, straight stitch, satin stitch, stem stitch and seed stitch.

DIRECTIONS

THE EMBROIDERY
▨ Trace the flower design and enlarge it to the required dimensions as shown on page 10. This is a complex design, and you may find that it helps if you number each square on both the smaller and larger grids when you are enlarging the pattern. Alternatively, you may prefer to concentrate on copying the main outlines accurately, filling in the smaller details by hand: your design may vary from the original, but only in minor respects.
▨ Using the photograph as a guide, transfer the motif to the corner of the fabric. Use the carbon paper method given on page 11 and position the design approximately 18in (45cm) in from the raw edges of the fabric.
▨ Working with the fabric stretched in the embroidery hoop,

embroider the large flowers and areas of foliage in long and short stitch and the clusters of smaller flowers in satin stitch. Work the stems in stem stitch and the grasses in seed stitch and straight stitch.
▨ Use the photograph and the design as a guide when blending the colors, and work with four strands of thread for solid color areas and for shaded areas.
▨ When the embroidery is finished, place the fabric face down on a well-padded surface and press it lightly, taking care not to crush the stitches.

FINISHING
▨ Following a line of the checker pattern, turn a double ¾in (2cm) hem to the wrong side all around. Either make straight folds at the corners, or cut away spare fabric diagonally and make mitered folds.
▨ Pin and stitch the hem in place

N/O   A/N

B, E, C, D

To enlarge the design, first draw a grid on tracing paper, each square measuring ¼in × ¼in (5mm × 5mm). Trace over the main outlines of the design, then enlarge it onto a 1in (2.5cm) grid. Fill in any details by hand and transfer the design to the fabric. The letters show which colors are used in particular areas: where two letters are given together, for example H/K, use two strands of each color in the needle.

KEY

A	927	M	819
B	642	N	415
C	3024	O	452
D	822	P	3051
E	369	R	3053
F	368	S	3032
G	776		
H	223		
J	335		
K	3354		
L	778		

SEASHELL TRACERY

The delicate traces of seashells are worked in white satin stitch on a padded panel of navy cotton chintz. The embroidered square is then bordered with navy-and-white-striped cotton and navy chintz – the entire panel is attached to a plain white cotton sheet to create a stylish bed throw.

MATERIALS

1½yd (1.5m) × 45in (115cm) wide navy blue cotton chintz	White dress marking chalk
2ft (60cm) × 2ft (60cm) polyester wadding	Knitting needle
	White sewing thread
2ft (60cm) × 2ft (60cm) fine calico	Chenille needle size 18 or 20
28in (70cm) × 36in (90cm) wide navy-and-white-striped cotton	Navy sewing thread
	White cotton sheet, single-bed size

Thread
2oz (50gm) ball of white knitting cotton, sport weight

Embroidery Stitch
Satin stitch

DIRECTIONS

▦ From the navy chintz cut out one square 24in (62cm) × 24½in (62cm) and four strips each 7½in (19cm) × 41in (103cm).

▦ From the striped cotton cut four strips 2¼in (5.5cm) × 25½in (64cm) wide, across the stripes.

▦ Enlarge the design to the dimensions given on the pattern.

▦ Pierce each small dot on the full-size pattern with the point of the knitting needle, then place the pattern over the chintz square and mark the dots on the right side of the fabric with the dress marking chalk.

▦ Place wadding between the chintz and the calico, making sure the chintz is right side up. There should be ⅜in (1cm) surplus of chintz all round the

square. Pin through the three layers to hold them in place before tacking together vertically and horizontally, using the white sewing thread.

▦ Embroider the dots in satin stitch with the knitting cotton. Then work the remaining motifs in the same way, using the diagram as a guide to the placement.

▦ Remove the tacking threads and press the ⅜in (1cm) surplus of chintz to the wrong side, taking care not to flatten the wadding.

▦ To make the narrow striped border, machine stitch the striped sections together at the corners as shown in the diagram using the navy thread.

▦ To make the wide chintz 'frame' machine stitch the chintz strips at the four angles shown in the diagram.

▦ Place the striped border

centered on the white sheet and pin it in position. Then put the embroidered chintz square in the center of the striped border and tack in position. Machine stitch around the edge of the square, keeping the stitches as close to the edge as possible. Remove the tacking thread.

▨ Turn and press a ⅜in (1cm) hem on the inner and outer edges of the chintz 'frame' and position it around the edge of the striped border, overlapping it by ⅜in (1cm) to hide the raw edges. Pin and then tack it in place. Machine stitch around the inner and outer edges of the 'frame', as close to the edge as possible. Remove the tacking stitches.

▨ Press the chintz frame and border carefully, but do not press the embroidered chintz square or the wadding will be flattened.

Taking inspiration from nature, the stylized forms of the shells above have been reproduced on the bed throw. By simplifying other natural forms, an endless variety of fascinating designs can be created.

The shell shapes are worked in dots and blocks of satin stitch on the central padded section. This is framed firstly by a narrow striped border and then by a wide, plain navy blue border.

169

VARIATIONS IN GREEN

In some hot countries, the people weave leafy branches above their beds to create a cool atmosphere: this tender green design could have the same soothing effect. It features fronds of the castor-oil plant, copied from a botanical drawing and worked in a wide range of greens to create a realistic effect. The design here is shown on a large pillow of a type not generally found outside France, so the quantities and dimensions quoted have been adjusted to make a standard single duvet cover.

Size 54in × 80in (136cm × 200cm).

MATERIALS

7yd (6.3m) of 56in (140cm) wide white fabric with an even weave	Dressmakers' carbon paper in a dark color
1yd (1m) of nylon snap tape	Crewel needle size 3 or 4
White sewing thread	Large embroidery hoop

Threads

DMC pearl cotton No. 5: two skeins each of **gray** 644, 647 and 648; **green** 320, 367, 368, 369, 469, 470, 471, 472, 500, 503, 504, 703, 904, 911, 954, 966, 987 and 989, and (optional) two skeins of DMC stranded cotton in **white** (if you wish to make a drawn-threadwork hem)

Embroidery stitches

Straight stitch, running stitch, stem stitch, Chinese knots, back stitch and hem stitch (optional).

DIRECTIONS

▦ The designer used an old cover with a drawn-threadwork pattern and superimposed her own design over this. The drawn-threadwork hem stitching is not an essential part of the design, and it would be simpler to omit the lines running straight across the leaf design. If you decide to keep the lines of drawn-threadwork which border the design and edge the frill, make these before beginning the leaf embroidery.

▦ Cut the two main pieces, each measuring 56in × 83¾in (140cm × 209.5cm) from the fabric. Cut the remaining fabric into 8in (20cm) wide strips and join these to make a continuous strip for the frill. Turn under and press a double ⅜in (1cm) hem along one edge. If you are not working a decorative edge, stitch the hem of the frill in the standard way.

▦ If you are working the hem-stitched borders, make them at this stage along the hem of the frill and running parallel to the sides of the main fabric piece, 6in (15cm) in from the raw edges, using the photograph as a guide to position. Stitch the borders in the same way as the border of the napkin on page 108, catching in the hem along the frill and making a purely decorative border (no hem) around the main fabric piece.

▦ Trace the leaf design and enlarge it to the required dimensions, following the instructions given on page 10. Using dressmakers' carbon paper, transfer the design to the center of the fabric.

▦ Working with the fabric stretched in the embroidery hoop and using the photograph as a color and stitch guide, embroider the leaf design mainly in straight stitch and running stitch,

strengthening the outlines with back stitch and stem stitch. Use Chinese knots to pick out the details on the seeds.

When the embroidery is finished, place the fabric face down on a well-padded surface and press it lightly, taking care not to crush the stitches.

FINISHING THE COVER

Divide the frill into four equal sections and mark with pins. Gather each frill section in turn.

Mark the central point on the *seam line* at each edge of the front section of the cover. The seam line is 3in (7.5cm) in from the raw edge along the bottom and ¾in (2cm) in along the remaining three sides.

Position the frill on the front, with right sides together and the finished edge of the frill lying inwards. The frill has a ⅝in (1.5cm) seam allowance, so match seam lines, not raw edges.

Matching marked points, pull up the gathering stitches of each section of the frill in turn. Pin and stitch the frill in place along the edges of the front.

Trim the seam allowance on the frill only to ¼in (6mm). Finish the cover as described for the cover on page 152, making sure that the frill lies inwards.

KEY

a	966	
b	504	
c	369	
d	368	
e	320	
f	367	
g	954	
h	472	

i	989
j	904
k	471
l	470
m	469
n	911
o	987
p	703

q	503
r	500
s	648
t	644
u	647

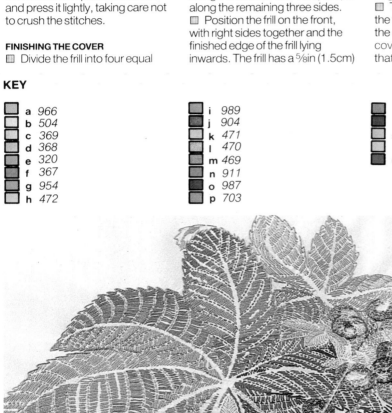

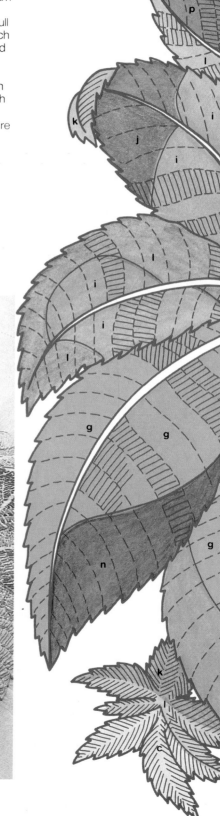

SPRINGTIME DREAM

This lavishly embroidered, luxuriously feminine bedcover, with its matching pillowcases, was inspired by four new varieties of tulip: Greenland, pink and tender green; Angélique, luscious as a peony; Shirley, ivory tinged with purple, and Dreaming Mead, with its lovely closed buds. You can either embroider the designs by hand, as seen in the picture, carefully blending the different shades like a skilled artist, or for quicker results you could machine embroider the flowers and leaves, using variegated threads. An even speedier method would be to paint the design, using fabric paints and taking care to make delicately shaded petals. The flowers, stems and leaves might be outlined in stem stitch and selected areas highlighted with satin stitching.

Size: bedcover 92in×87in (230cm×220cm); pillowcases 36in×24¾in (90cm×62cm), including scalloped edges.

MATERIALS

4¼yd (3.8m) of 90in (228cm) wide fine cotton or linen fabric
*DMC stranded cotton as follows: two skeins each of **green** 92, 369 and 703, and **ecru**; one skein each of **green** 94, 471, 472, 580, 966, 987, 989 and 3347, **white**, **pink** 62, 106, 112, 602, 603, 604, 760, 761, 776, 819, 892, 893, 948, 3326 and 3689, **blue** 828 and **yellow** 445*
or machine embroidery cottons in variegated pinks and greens
or fabric paints and a range of paint brushes with green and
pink stranded cottons for outlining the designs
*2 reels of DMC machine embroidery cotton in **pale pink** No. 50, for scalloped edges of pillowcases*
Pink colored pencil
Crewel needle size 7 or 8
Tracing paper
Dressmakers' carbon paper
Large embroidery hoop
Matching thread
Note *If the above yarn is unobtainable, refer to page 191.*

DIRECTIONS

▦ Cut one piece of fabric 98in (246cm) long, cutting across the full width, for the bedcover. For the pillowcases, cut two pieces 36in×24¾in (90cm×62cm) for the tops and two pieces 36in×20in (90cm×50cm) for the bottoms.

▦ On the bedcover piece, make ¾in (2cm) double hems down the sides, and 1½in (4cm) double hems at the top and bottom.

▦ Starting from the corners measure out evenly spaced scallops around the edges of the pillowcase tops and draw them on the fabric in colored pencil. Embroider the scallops in pink machine embroidery cotton,

using machine satin stitch ³⁄₁₆in (4mm) wide.

▦ Enlarge the design for the bedcover onto tracing paper and transfer it to the cover with dressmakers' carbon paper (see page 11), using the photograph as a guide to position.

▦ Transfer the pillowcase design to the pillowcase tops in the same manner.

▦ Embroider the tulip motifs in long and short stitch, using the charts as color guides and the photograph as a stitch guide. Two strands of thread are used throughout and the stitches should be between ⅛in (3mm) and ³⁄₁₆in (4mm) long to achieve the painted effect shown on the photograph. Work with the fabric

stretched in an embroidery hoop, moving it as necessary.

▦ If you wish to work the design in machine embroidery, first stitch the main outlines by hand in stem stitch. Then put the fabric in a small embroidery hoop: lay the fabric right side up over the outer ring, then place the inner ring over it, so the fabric can lie flat on the base plate of your machine. Set the machine to straight running stitch and make the feed inoperative so that you can move the ring freely until each area is filled with stitching. The speed with which you move the ring about will govern the length of the stitches, so practise first.

▦ When the embroidery is complete, place it face

downwards on a well-padded surface and press it lightly, taking care not to crush the stitches.

▦ To complete the pillowcases, for each pillowcase take an bottom section and make ⅜in (1cm) double hems down all four sides. Bring over a 4¾in (12cm) deep fold of fabric to the wrong side across one short end and tack at the sides.

▦ With wrong sides together, center bottom section over pillowcase top, taking care that scalloped edges extend evenly all around. Pin and tack together, then topstitch or stabstitch along the two long sides and the unfolded short end. Remove tacking and insert pillow, tucking it under the flap.

Enlarge to twice this size (see page 10).

Enlarge to twice this size (see page 10).

Enlarge to twice this size
(see page 10).

KEY

Top left

a	948	**n**	989	**h**	white	**d** 3347
b	112	**o**	987	**i**	828	**e** 369
c	106	**p**	472	**j**	948	**f** 819
d	62	**q**	966	**k**	989	**g** 776
e	776	**r**	92	**l**	987	**h** 471
f	761			**m**	445	**i** 3689
g	760	Bottom left		**n**	472	**j** 948
h	893	**a**	602	**o**	966	**k** 760
i	892	**b**	603	**p**	92	**l** 761
j	3326	**c**	604			**m** 604
k	819	**d**	819	Above		**n** 471
l	white	**e**	776	**a**	ecru	**o** 94
m	369	**f**	ecru	**b**	white	**p** 703
		g	369	**c**	3326	**q** 92

r	603
s	472
t	966
u	580

177

CEREMONIAL CHIC

Create a family heirloom by working on the best of materials: a beautiful damask tablecloth, woven with a geometric design. Each square is filled with finely worked circles, triangles and bars in shiny pastels, with zigzags and bars and bows and knots. You could adapt the idea too – wavy lines or circles worked round the damask motifs of any beautiful old linen cloth will be just as original. Or embroider a beautiful length of fabric to make a party skirt or dance frock.

MATERIALS

White and silver cotton damask fabric, to make a cloth. (Alternatively, the silver lines can be added to white fabric by machine zigzag lines across the length and width of the fabric, using a fine metallic machine thread.)
Crewel needle size 6 or 7
Crewel needle size 4
HB pencil
Embroidery hoop

Threads
Susan Bates Anchor stranded cotton in the following colors:
blue 128, 130; **green** 187, 238, 253; **kingfisher blue** 433; **turquoise** 185; **pale tan** 347; **yellow** 292, 297; **pink** 48, 54, 968; **gray** 397; **cream** 386; **beige** 830
DMC **fil d'argent** 280

Embroidery Stitches
Satin stitch, straight stitch, cross stitch, knots (see diagram).

DIRECTIONS

▦ Use the photographs as a guide to the placement of the motifs and for the colors. Draw the circles, squares and triangles lightly on the fabric with the HB pencil.

▦ Work with the fabric stretched in an embroidery hoop, moving the hoop as each section is completed.

▦ Embroider the circles, squares and triangles in satin stitch using three strands of thread and the finer crewel needle; take care to cover the pencil lines completely.

▦ Work the zigzags and bars at random (without pencil guidelines which would be difficult to conceal) in straight stitch, using either three strands of cotton or one strand of silver thread.

▦ Next, add the cross stitch and the 'V' shapes in straight stitch, again using three strands of cotton or one of silver.

▦ Place the cloth face down on a well-padded surface and press lightly, taking care not to crush the stitches.

▦ Then add the 'bows' by making simple knots, as shown in the diagram, with either six strands of cotton or two strands of silver thread.

▦ To make up the cloth, turn a double hem all round (see page 14 for instructions on mitering corners) and either machine or hand stitch.

The 'bows' – knotted and cut threads.

traditional wedding cloth with a modern gloss

Multi-sized circles in a haphazard arrangement are satin-stitched in a variety of hues.

Mix squares, circles and triangles, completing the design with zigzag of color.

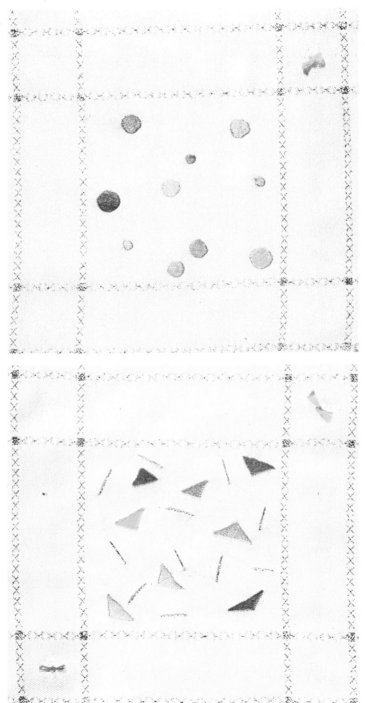

Different colored triangles are interspersed with bars of silver, which match the cross stitching.

Small groups of pastel-colored squares, straight or slanted, make for a pleasing arrangement.

Just triangles in bright colors all the same size. Match up with thread bows at the corners.

Pick three colors and make up thread bows to fill the square. Add silver cross stitches.

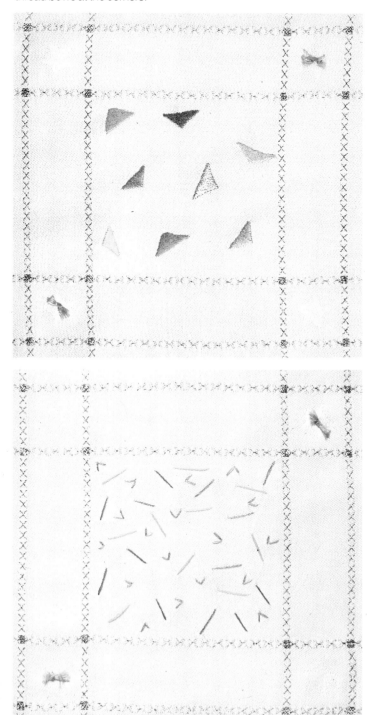
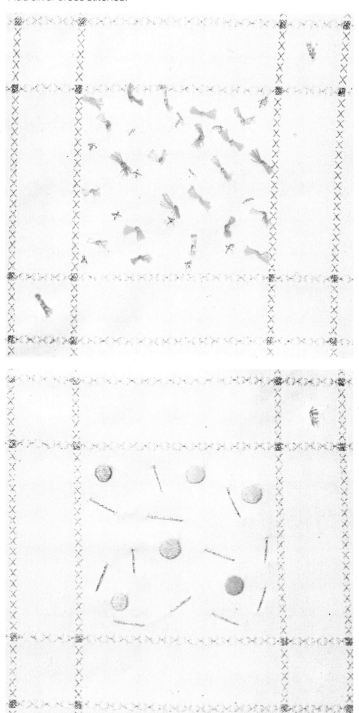

Stitched bars of yellow and blue mingle with green 'V'-shapes. Complete with thread bows.

Similar-sized circles in pastel shades are split up by bars of silver.

GEOMETRIC PERFECTION

Dark blue embroidery on pure white cotton piqué makes an elegant and unusual floor covering, visually interesting yet at the same time in perfect harmony with the cool, uncluttered modern style. White cotton might seem impractical as a floor covering – and indeed you could equally well use this as a wall hanging or a bed throw – but it is machine washable. If you have time to spare, you could even embroider a kimono to match.

Size: 52in × 52in (130cm × 130cm).

MATERIALS

3yd (2.7m) of 54in (135cm) wide
white cotton piqué
3yd (2.7m) of 36in (90cm) wide
lightweight polyester padding
DMC coton à broder: 35 skeins of

***blue** 2336*
Tracing paper
Dressmakers' carbon paper
Matching thread

DIRECTIONS

▦ Cut two pieces of cotton piqué, each measuring 53½in × 53½in (133cm × 133cm). Also cut two lengths of padding, each 52in (130cm) long

▦ Place the strips of padding side by side and herringbone stitch the edges together. Turn the pieces the other way up and repeat the process. Trim the resulting piece of padding to measure 52in × 52in (130cm × 130cm).

▦ Draw a grid on tracing paper and scale up the design. Position the tracing paper over the center of one fabric square, on the right side of the fabric, and pin both fabric and paper to a flat surface, pinning around the edge of the design. Slide the carbon paper, coated side down, between the fabric and the paper design. Because of the scale of the design, you may find it necessary to work section by section. Trace over the design, marking it on the fabric.

▦ Leaving an even ⅝in (1.5cm) margin of cotton piqué all around, pin and tack the polyester padding to the wrong side of the marked cotton. Place the padded and unpadded cotton squares with right sides together and pin, tack and stitch together

around the outer edge, taking a ⅝in (1.5cm) seam allowance and leaving a gap for turning.

▦ Turn the square right side out, enclosing the padding. Fold in seam allowances along the gap and slipstitch to close.

▦ Smooth out the three layers and make lines of tacking across the fabric, vertically and horizontally, at intervals of about 4in (10cm), taking care not to ruckle the layers.

▦ Using three strands of embroidery cotton in your needle, embroider the design. The dots marked A consist of a cluster of seven French knots, as shown on page 184. The section of the design marked B is worked in a graduated satin stitch. It is not essential that all stitches should pass through all three layers, but the layers should be held together at intervals of approximately 4in (10cm), or the finished mat may tend to ruckle.

▦ When the central design is complete, topstitch all around the mat in matching thread, ¾in (2cm) from the outer edge.

▦ Using three strands of embroidery cotton, complete the design with diagonal lines of large darning stitches across the undecorated section, stitching through all layers and finishing off neatly.

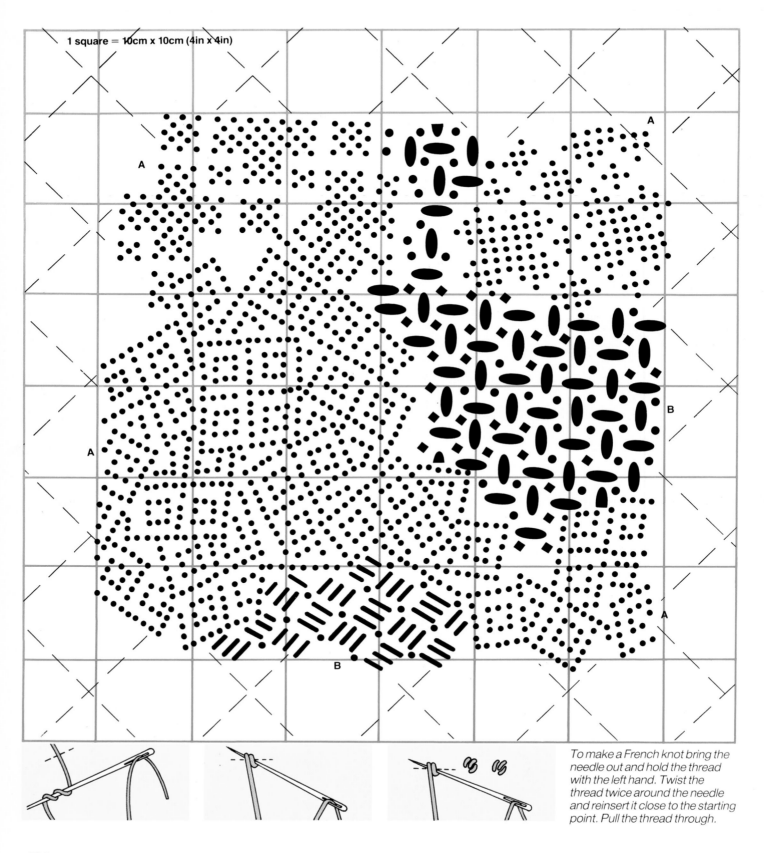

1 square = 10cm x 10cm (4in x 4in)

To make a French knot bring the needle out and hold the thread with the left hand. Twist the thread twice around the needle and reinsert it close to the starting point. Pull the thread through.

The pattern shown opposite can equally be applied to a shirt (or kimono) as to a rug. The color scheme has been reversed (above), to striking effect.

CHINA BLUE, POPPY RED

Blue-and-white porcelain vases are filled with the glorious tulips and poppies of late spring and early summer. Noone would pretend that these luxurious cushion covers are the sort of thing that you can complete in a day, but there is a great deal of pleasure to be gained from working with such a rich, lustrous and varied range of colors, and even more satisfaction to come, when your friends compliment you on the finished cushions.

Size Approximately 24in × 24in (60cm × 60cm).

MATERIALS

FOR ONE COVER
1½yd (1.4m) of 36in (90cm) wide closely woven white cotton fabric
Matching sewing thread
Crewel needle size 6 or 7

Large embroidery hoop
Tracing paper
Dressmakers' carbon paper
16in (40cm) zipper

Threads
FOR THE TULIP CUSHION
*DMC stranded cotton: one skein each of **pink** 353, 604, 605, 776, 778, 818, 962, 3326 and 3684, **yellow** 742, 743, 744, 972 and 973, **flesh** 948, **orange** 741, **peach** 754,*

***apricot** 352, **white, ecru, gray beige** 644, **wine** 814, **green** 320, 368, 703, 987, 988 and 989, **mauve** 316, and **blue** 800, and three skeins of **blue** 798*

FOR THE POPPY CUSHION
*DMC stranded cotton: one skein each of **wine** 814, 3685 and 902, **orange** 741 and 947, **apricot** 350 and 351, **blue** 800, **yellow** 725 and 742, **black** 310, **green** 703, 704,*

*904, 906, 907, 988 and 989, **rust** 817, and **pink** 353; two skeins each of **red** 321 and 498, **orange** 608, and **apricot** 352; three skeins of **blue** 798, and four skeins each of **red** 606 and 666*

Embroidery stitches
TULIP CUSHION
Long and short stitch, satin stitch, stem stitch and chain stitch.

POPPY CUSHION
Long and short stitch, satin stitch, stem stitch and Chinese knots.

DIRECTIONS

TULIP CUSHION
▦ Cut a 28in × 28in (70cm × 70cm) square of cotton fabric. Cut two more pieces, each 25¼in × 13¼in (63cm × 33cm) and set these aside.
▦ Scale up the design on tracing paper and transfer it to the center of the fabric square, using dressmakers' carbon paper (see page 11).

▦ Work with the fabric stretched in an embroidery hoop, moving it as necessary. Three strands of thread are used throughout.
▦ Embroider the tulips and leaves in long and short stitch and the stems in satin stitch, using the chart as a color guide. No two people would reproduce this design exactly the same, stitch for stitch; the important thing is to embroider each petal separately, making sure that the color

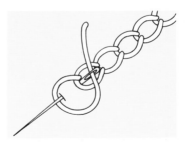

chain stitch

changes blend gradually into each other, to give the effect of the subtle variations of tone to be found on flower petals.
▦ Work the vase mainly in satin stitch, picking out the details in stem stitch and the arabesques in chain stitch, using the photograph as a stitch guide.
▦ When the embroidery is complete, place it face down on a well-padded surface and press it lightly, taking care not to crush the stitches. Trim to measure 25¼in (63cm) square.
▦ Take the other two pieces of cotton fabric and place them right sides together. Pin and tack together down one long side, taking a ⅝in (1.5cm) seam allowance. At either side, stitch from the raw edge towards the center for 4⅝in (11.5cm), leaving a gap for the zipper. Insert zipper.
▦ With right sides together and zipper open, pin, tack and stitch cushion back to cushion front, around all the outside and taking a ⅝in (1.5cm) seam allowance. Turn right side out.

POPPY CUSHION
▦ Cut fabric, scale up and transfer design as for tulip cushion. Work with the fabric in an embroidery hoop, using three strands of cotton throughout.
▦ Embroider the flowers in long and short stitch and the stems in satin stitch, using the chart as a color guide. Pick out the poppy seeds in Chinese knots, using black thread. Work the vase mainly in satin stitch, with stem stitch for the linear details, using the photograph as a stitch guide.
▦ Press the finished embroidery and make up the cushion cover as for the tulip cushion.

KEY FOR TULIP CUSHION

a	*353*	**q**	*352*
b	*604*	**r**	*white*
c	*605*	**s**	*ecru*
d	*776*	**t**	*644*
e	*778*	**u**	*814*
f	*818*	**v**	*320*
g	*3326*	**w**	*368*
h	*368*	**x**	*987*
i	*742*	**y**	*988*
j	*743*	**z**	*989*
k	*744*	**A**	*316*
l	*972*	**B**	*800*
m	*973*	**C**	*798*
n	*948*	**D**	*445*
o	*741*	**E**	*307*
p	*754*	**F**	*602*

KEY FOR POPPY CUSHION

a	*814*	**n**	*906*
b	*3685*	**o**	*817*
c	*741*	**p**	*321*
d	*947*	**q**	*608*
e	*350*	**r**	*352*
f	*351*	**s**	*353*
g	*800*	**t**	*798*
h	*725*	**u**	*606*
i	*742*	**v**	*666*
j	*310*	**w**	*743*
k	*703*	**x**	*922*
l	*704*		
m	*904*		

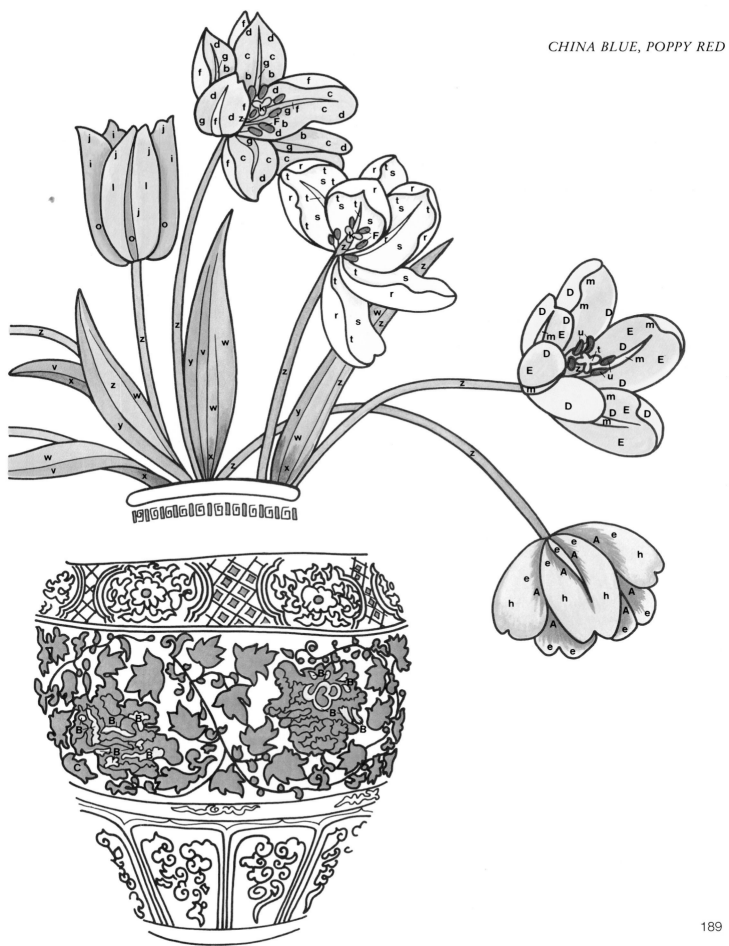

STOCKISTS

DMC Yarns
DMC Corporation 107 Trumbull Street
Elizabeth NJ 07206 (201) 351-4550

Mail order companies:

Anchor Yarns
Susan Bates, Inc. 212 Middlesex Avenue
Chester, CT 06412 (203) 526-5381

Merino Wool Co., Inc
230 Fifth Avenue New York NY 10001 (212) 686-0050

Pingouin Yarns
P.O. Box 100 Jamestown SC 29453 1-800-845-2291

ACKNOWLEDGMENTS

2	Burgi/Lebeau
5	Duffas/Garcon
6	Godeaut/Faver
7 top left	Dirand/Lebeau
7 top right	Bouchet/Lebeau
7 below	Tisne/Garcon
8-9	Dirand/Lebeau
11	Laiter/Garcon
12	Bouchet/Chabaneix
13 top left	Bouchet/Lebeau
13 top right	Duffas/Garcon
16-17	Dirand/Lebeau
18-20	M Duffas/J Schoumacher
23-26	B Maltaverne/C Lebeau
27-28	M Duffas/I Garcon
30-33	M Duffas/I Garcon
34-35	J Dirand/C Lebeau
39	M Duffas/I Garcon
42-44	M Duffas/I Garcon
46-47	A Bianchi/I Garcon
49	G De Chabaneix/A Lurtz
52	N Bruant/C Lebeau
53	C Lebeau/Lebeau
56-57	B Maltaverne/Marion Faver
60-61	B Maltaverne/C Lebeau
64-65	Tisne/Garcon
66-67	E Novick/I Garcon
69	M Duffas/I Garcon
70-71	M Duronsoy/A Jacobs
72-73	J Tisne/I Garcon
76-77	J Tisne/I Garcon
78-79	J P Godeaut/M Faver
80-81	A Bianchi/I Garcon
84-85	B Maltaverne/C Lebeau
86-87	Bouchet/Lebeau
88-89	M Duffas/I Garcon
91	G Bouchet/C Lebeau
92-95	M Duffas/J Schoumacher
96-99	M Duffas/J Schoumacher
100-101	G. de Chabaneix/C Lebeau
102-105	G Bouchet/C de Chabaneix
106-107	M Duffas/J Schoumacher
109	J Dirand/C Lebeau
110-111	M Duffas/I Garcon
114-115	B Maltaverne/C Lebeau
116-121	M Duffas/I Garcon
122-123	M Duffas/J Schoumacher
124-129	J Dirand/C Lebeau
130-133	V Assenat/J Schoumacher
134-137	B Maltaverne/C Lebeau
138-141	D de Chabaneix/I Garcon
143-145	Duffas/Schoumacher/Garcon
146-147	Duffas/Garcon
150-151	Duffas/Schoumacher
152-156	Chabaneix/Garcon
158-160	Chabaneix/Chabaneix
162-163	Duffas/Schoumacher
164-166	Assenat/Schoumacher
168-169	Bruant/Lebeau
170-172	Bouchet/Lebeau
174-175	Chabaneix/Garcon
180-181	Bianchi/Garcon
182-183	Burgi/Lebeau
184-185	Burgi/Lebeau
186-188	Dirand/Lebeau

Family Circle's

Treasury of
Needlework
Stitches

By
Jacqueline Enthoven
May 1971

Jacqueline Enthoven *is one of the country's leading needlework authorities and author of* The Stitches of Creative Embroidery (*published by Van Nostrand Reinhold*). *Working with the editors of* Family Circle, *she has compiled this special 1971 Treasury with over 50 step-by-step illustrations of the most popular embroidery and needlepoint stitches, and a detailed description of the technique and suggested uses for each stitch. We're sure you will want to clip it out and save it as a handy reference.*

This valuable guide will serve as a primer for the beginner, a refresher for the more experienced needleworker and an inspiration to all to learn, to experiment, to try new combinations and to create your own designs. Try stitches that you have never worked before. Repeat several rows close together, for instance, and then adapt the pattern to interpret an idea you have developed. Try threading your stitches; it is one of the easiest ways to create something spontaneously. ❦ In this section, the embroidery stitches are grouped in five categories, according to the way they are made. The *flat-stitch* family, which is the largest, forms the first group. The stitches lie flat on the surface of the cloth, either close together or spaced. Flat stitches with a curve or loop become *looped stitches*. Closing the loop makes *chained stitches*. Twisting and tightening the loops make *knotted stitches*. The last section comprises some of the most popular *needlepoint* stitches. ❦ For materials, we suggest a No. 16, 17 or 18 tapestry needle (that is, a needle without a sharp point); a yarn in your favorite color (for a beginner, pearl cotton works well, as it does not separate or become fuzzy and gives a crisp definition). Or, use No. 3- or No. 4-ply worsted yarn. Choose a loosely woven fabric, such as homespun, linen or burlap. Use an embroidery hoop, if you wish, or spray the back of the fabric with spray starch for added stiffness. ❦ For needlepoint, use No. 10-mesh single- or double-thread needlepoint canvas, tapestry needle and tapestry wool. ❦ After you have become more confident you will want to try a variety of materials for texture and contrast, and very often the materials you use will determine the direction of your design. ❦ Raid your sewing basket for supplies and begin to work right now! Transfer your finished design to a pillow, a wall hanging, clothing, accessories, or make a decorative sampler of your favorite stitches—as we've done on the facing page.

FLAT STITCHES

1. Running Stitch—Runs in and out of the cloth at regular intervals.

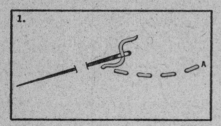

2. Darning Stitch—Picks up very little cloth with the needle. Most of the yarn stays on the front of the work.

These two simple stitches form the basis for countless exciting variations. Try as many as you can, varying the size of your stitches and the weight of the yarn.

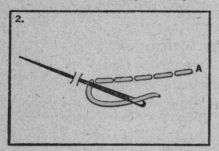

3. Double Running Stitch—Used for a solid line. After you have worked a row of regular *running stitches* (1) from right to left, turn your work around at the end of the row and stitch back, filling the gaps. You can use a different shade of the same color.

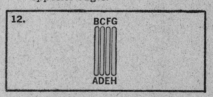

4. Pattern Darning—Another way to make borders and fill shapes. It is made up of rows of *darning stitches* (2) of varying lengths worked into definite patterns. We suggest a border made up of 3 to 5 rows of regular *darning stitches* worked very close together, checkerboard fashion.

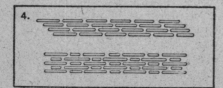

5. Back Stitch—A useful stitch for a crisp outline. It is good for stitchery lettering. Work from right to left. From A take a stitch backwards to B, coming out at C in front of A. Go back in at A, out at D, back to C, *etc.*

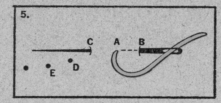

6. Seed or Dot Stitch—When you need a light airy effect, use small *back stitches* (5) placed in patterns or at random. To make a double seed stitch, make 2 *back stitches* in the same hole, neatly relaxed, side by side.

RUNNING, DARNING, BACK AND SEED STITCHES—Can be whipped, threaded and double-threaded. They are effective for outlines and produce interesting textures when several rows are close together. The same yarn can be used, or different weights or colors, to produce a variety of effects. Some of these can be worked quickly as a border on a table mat, a cushion, or around a skirt.

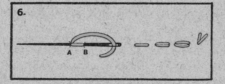

7. Whipped Running

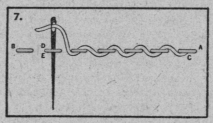

8. Double-threaded Running

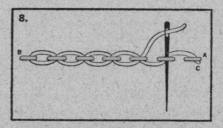

9. Threaded Checkerboard Running

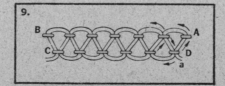

10. Threaded Zigzag Darning

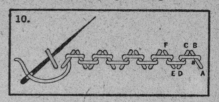

11. Satin Stitch—Made up of *back stitches* (5) worked side by side to cover a shape. It is sometimes difficult to work a neat edge. One remedy is to cover the edge with *stem* (21), *back* (5) or *chain* (34) stitches.

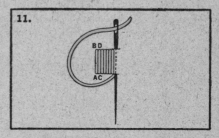

12. Surface Satin Stitch—This stitch has the same effect as the one above but requires less yarn. Instead of going to the back and around as for regular *satin stitch* (11), most of the yarn stays on the surface of the cloth; very small stitches are picked up on opposite edges.

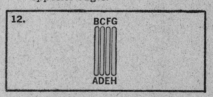

13. Straight (Stroke) Stitches—These are easy to work. They can be the same or different lengths going freely in any direction you want. They can also be worked in rows or geometric patterns. If they are too long, tie them down with *back stitches* (5).

14. Threaded Straight Stitches—One of the best ways to learn to create spontaneously with stitches is to thread *straight stitches* (13). It leads to many interesting designs such as growing forms, grasses, exciting circular shapes, quick and easy flowers. Start with a *straight stitch* from A to B. Come out at C and thread under AB, insert at D. Continue threading under either CB or DB.

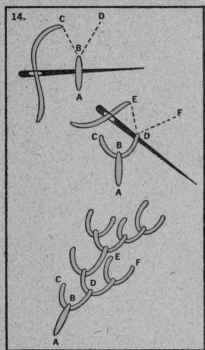

15. Cloud Filling—Another way of creating interesting effects by threading. First work a foundation of small, spaced, upright stitches. Thread the first and second rows together, then second and third rows, *etc.*

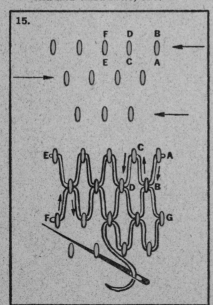

16. Wave Stitch—This is another threaded stitch which covers a shape quickly. Start with a row of small upright stitches worked across the top of the shape to be filled: AB—CD—EF. At the end of the row, from H go under to I and thread under HG, in at J, out at K under the next upright, *etc.*

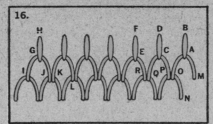

17. Cross Stitch—Made with 2 *straight stitches* (13) of equal size crossing each other diagonally. They can be worked individually going from D under, back to C to start another cross, or they can be worked in rows.

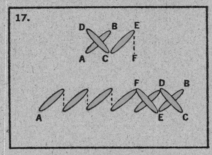

18. Upright Cross—This stitch makes a good filling.

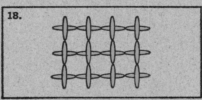

19. Star Stitch—A double *cross stitch*, that is, a regular *cross stitch* (17) with an *upright cross stitch* (18) worked over it, to which a small *cross stitch* is added on each side of the vertical stitch.

20. Cross Stitch Flower—A decorative *cross stitch* variation. It can be used in individual units or massed in groups. Work *2 cross stitches* (17) on top of each other, in the same holes. On the way back to D, with the point of the needle, and without picking up any cloth, go over the last stitch EF and under AB, or if AB presents itself first, under AB and over EF. You are weaving over and under, or under and over. Insert at D.

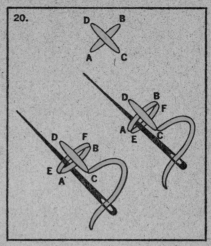

21. Stem or Crewel and Outline—Used for lines or as a filling by working rows closely side by side. Come out at A. Holding the thread down with your left thumb, insert the needle at B. Come out at C, halfway between AB. Over to D, still with the thread down, out at B, over to E and out at D, *etc.* When the yarn is kept *down*, the stitch is called a *stem* or *crewel*. When the yarn is kept *above* the line, it is called an *outline stitch*, the line looking straighter.

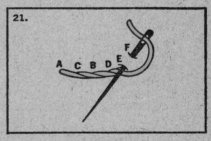

22. Alternating Stem Stitch—This stitch is worked like the *stem stitch* (21) from left to right. But instead of being held down for every stitch, the yarn is held alternately down for the first stitch from A to B, up for the second from C to D, down for the third, *etc.* A beautiful line is obtained by working 2 rows close to each other, the second reversing the first.

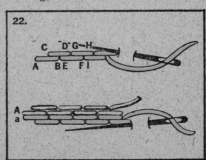

23. Herringbone—Once you master it, the herringbone is a stitch you can use in many different ways. Think in terms of a square with AB bisecting the square, going under to C, halfway back to the left. D is diagonally down, halfway across the next square as shown in the diagram.

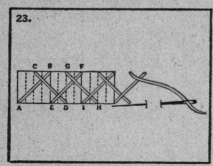

24. Threaded Herringbone—Threading a *herringbone stitch* (23) will surprise you. It is easy to do and very effective. Try using a contrasting color yarn. After you have worked a row of *herringbone*, bring the needle out at A. Lace over the crossed threads and under the slanting stitches without going through the cloth, except when you start and end.

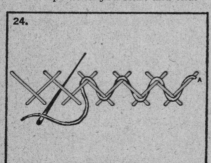

25. Double Herringbone—This stitch makes an effective border, especially if 2 colors are used. Two rows of *herringbone* (23) are worked over each other so that they interlace. The second color is laced under the first color on the way up, and over it on the way down.

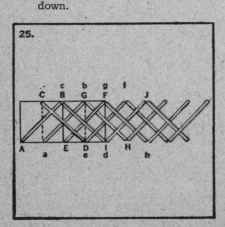

LOOPED STITCHES

26. Buttonhole or Blanket Stitch—The only difference is that *buttonhole stitches* are closer together. Work from left to right. Come out at A. Hold the yarn down with your left thumb, insert the needle at B. Come out at C, just above and close to A, drawing the needle out over the yarn coming from A to form a loop. In at D, out at E, *etc.*

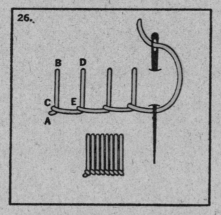

27. Closed Buttonhole Stitch—Made up of 2 *buttonhole stitches* (26) worked from the same hole, the first one from right to left, the second from left to right, making little triangles.

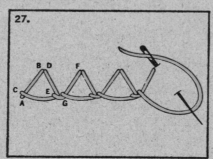

28. Double Buttonhole Stitch—For this effective border, work 2 rows of *blanket stitches* (26) facing each other. First work 1 row from left to right. At the end of the row, turn your work around and work the second row, fitting in between the arms of the first row.

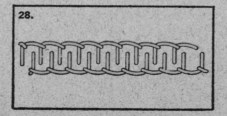

---

29. Single Feather Stitch—A good stitch for textured outlines. It is really a *blanket stitch* (26) with the stitches slanting instead of at right angles. Work from the top down, towards you.

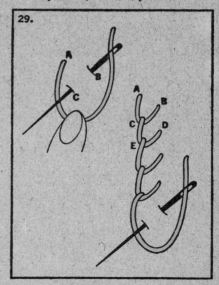

30. Slanting Feather Stitch—The best known of the feather stitch family. It is used for lines and for borders. Think in terms of working on 4 parallel lines and follow the diagram. Use it as a base for spontaneous stitching, adding stitches such as *detached chains* (35), *long stemmed knots* (42), or threading around each of the stitch ends.

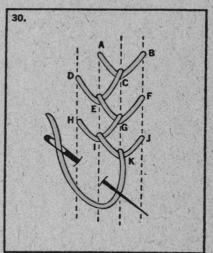

31. Cretan Stitch—Well worth the effort to learn and practice because it has many uses. It is a beautiful border stitch and is good for filling shapes as it adapts easily to various widths. It is a looped stitch, somewhat like a *blanket stitch* (26) worked first on one side then the other, except that instead of coming out on a center line, the stitches come out on 2 parallel lines. Note that the needle always points from outside in with the yarn under the needle.

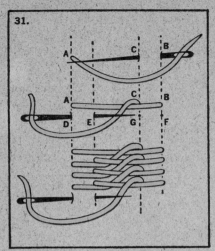

31.

32. Fly Stitch—Can be used in many ways. Make beautiful borders by having the stitches holding hands, back to back or facing each other. You can also overlap them. Bring the needle out at A. Hold the yarn down with the left thumb, looping it towards the right. Insert at B, coming out at C, below, halfway between A and B. The yarn is looped under the point of the needle from left to right. Pull it through over the loop. Anchor down by inserting at D. You can anchor it with a small stitch, or a long one, or with a *detached chain* (35).

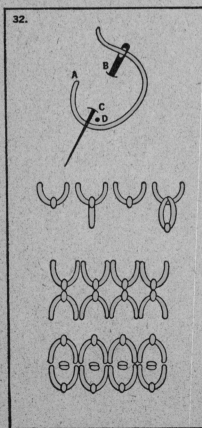

32.

33. Crown Stitch—A *fly stitch* (32) with an extra stitch on each side.

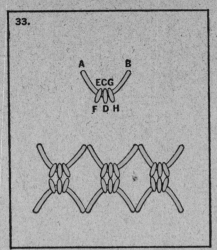

33.

CHAINED STITCHES

34. Chain Stitch—This is one of the most satisfying ways to follow an outline or to fill a shape. It also can be worked on canvas. Bring the needle out at A. Holding the yarn down with the left thumb, loop it towards the right. Insert the needle in the same hole at A and come out at B, with the yarn under the point of the needle from left to right. Draw the needle through. Repeat, inserting the needle at B inside the chain, in the same hole, keeping the yarn looped down from left to right. Come out at C, *etc.* At the end of the row, anchor the last chain down with a little stitch just below the last loop.

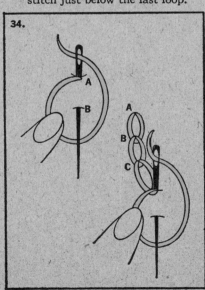

34.

35. Detached Chain—Instead of a row of chains, each chain can be

by itself, anchored with a small stitch at the bottom of the loop. It is also called "lazy daisy" and is useful for petals of flowers.

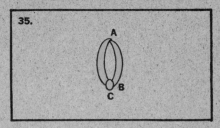

35.

36. Broad Chain or Threaded Chain—Many people, especially children, prefer this stitch to plain chain stitch. It is easier to work and follows curves beautifully. First take a small stitch from A to B Come out at C. Now pass the needle behind the stitch AB from right to left "under the bridge" without picking up any cloth. Insert again at C, out at D. Pull through gently so that the stitches will be relaxed. Slide the needle behind the chain BC, insert at D, out at E, *etc.*

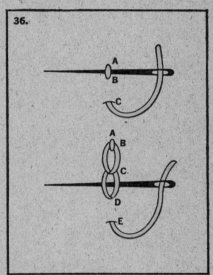

36.

Chain Stitch Variations—There are many ideas you can use to vary *chain stitches*. You can vary the length of the stitches. For some variations try introducing a different color or texture. Work *running* (1) or *back stitches* (5) in the middle or add a second row of chains on top of the first. Fill the chains with *seed stitches* (6), *French knots* (41), or work straight or slanting stitches over the sides. Chains can be whipped on one side or both sides, or the whole chain can be whipped.

37. Twisted Chain—This gives a different, somewhat knotted texture to a line. Work it as a *chain stitch* (34) but instead of always inserting the needle in the same hole, insert it to the left and take a slanting stitch from B to C.

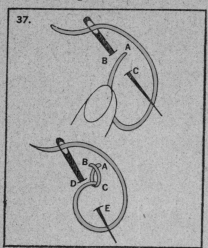

37.

38. Threaded Square Chain—It makes interesting borders, can be increased and decreased with ease. It can also be used for *couching* (45) heavy yarns. Start with 2 parallel *straight stitches* (13), AB–CD like the top and bottom of a square. If you like, you can add a *straight stitch* from B to C. From D, go under to E. Slide the needle upward under the 2 bridges DC and AB, without picking up any cloth. Insert at F, come out at G; pull through gently, not tightly. Slide the needle upward under ED and FA, insert at H, out at I, *etc.*

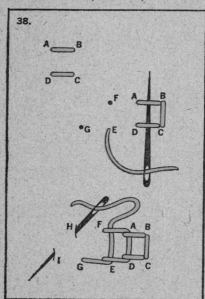

38.

39. Vandyke Stitch—Very much like the *threaded square chain* (38), except that the stitches are crossed instead of straight. Work it relaxed or keep the cloth taut in a hoop or frame. The needle slides under the crossed stitches without picking up any cloth. Once you understand the rhythm of the stitch, it goes very quickly.

Try it first starting with a *cross stitch* (17), with stitches close together: You get a raised braid useful for heavy lines. Then try to work it freely with arms swinging to one side or the other, or both sides. The width can be varied to fill spaces. It is a good stitch to play with on your doodling cloth.

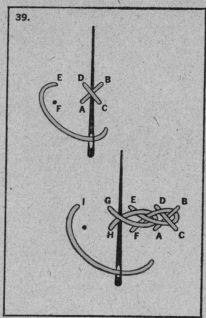

39.

40. Chained Cross Stitch—A more interesting texture than plain *cross stitch* (17) and goes just as quickly. Bring the needle out at A, insert diagonally at B, coming out at C. From C make a *chain stitch* (34) to D. Start again from D to E.

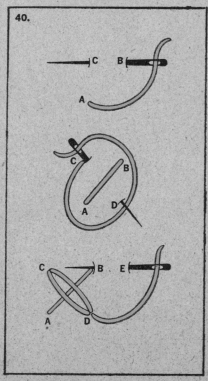

40.

41. French Knot—The easiest way to learn to make a good *French knot* is to have the cloth stretched taut in a hoop or on a frame, and to use heavy yarns. Bring the needle out at A. Swing your yarn to the left of A, circle it down from left to right and hold it flat on the cloth with your left thumb at a place about an inch to the left of A. With your right hand, hold the needle by the eye and slide the point downward "under the bridge", without picking up any cloth. Now think of a clock: Your needle should be pointing to 6 o'clock. Still holding the needle by the eye, turn the point of the needle clockwise, over the yarn held by your left thumb, until it points to 12 o'clock. Continue to hold the yarn down with your left thumb. Insert the point of the needle very close to A but not in the same hole. Now gently pull the yarn with your left thumb and index finger to snug it around the needle. Push the needle straight down with your right hand and pull through gently. If you want bigger knots, use 2 or 3 yarns at the same time; try several shades of the same color in your needle.

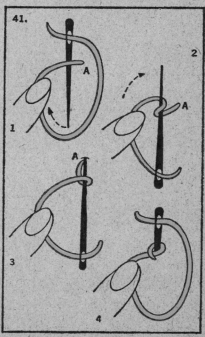

41.

42. Long-stemmed Knot—Useful for small flowers and many designs. Start exactly as for a regular *French knot* (41). When your needle points at 12 o'clock, slide it sideways to where you want the knot to be and insert there, leaving a stem.

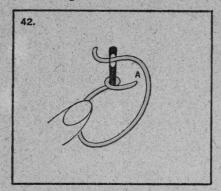

43. Coral Knot—Follows lines easily and gives them a decorative, nubby texture. The knots can be quite close together or spaced. Work from right to left. The yarn from A goes over the needle, then it is looped under the point, from left to right. *Coral knots* also can be worked in a zigzag.

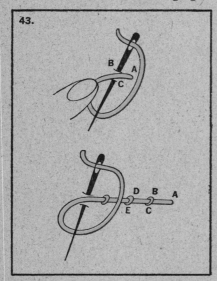

44. Palestrina Knot or Double Knot—This beautiful stitch produces a very decorative line. Use a heavy yarn and work the stitches close enough so they appear as a row of pearls. Work from left to right. Bring the needle out at A on the line to be covered. Take a small slanting stitch, inserting at B above the line, coming out at C below the line. The distance BC should equal AB for well-rounded knots close together. Slip the needle from above, under the AB stitch, without picking up any cloth. Pull through. Slip the needle from above under the first stitch again, to the right of the first slipped yarn which now goes under the needle, making a *buttonhole stitch* (26). Pull the yarn gently so that it encircles the first stitch. Start the next

slanting stitch to the right, inserting at D, coming out at E. DE equals BD.

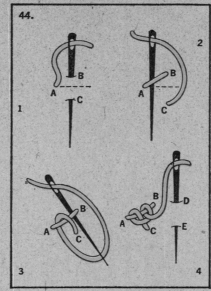

45. Couching—One of the oldest stitches in the world. It is very useful if you want to use yarns that are too thick or too fragile to go through the cloth easily. It is one of the best approaches to creating spontaneously with stitches, expressing a feeling or an idea. You will find it easiest if the cloth is held taut. Pull the beginning of the yarn you want to couch through to the back and lay it over the line you have in mind. Tack it down with another yarn. Besides the usual small even stitches, try couching with other stitches to vary the effect.

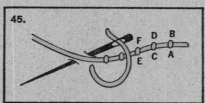

46. Roumanian Stitch —Good for broad lines and fillings. The same yarn is used for both couching and tying. Bring the needle out at A, go in at B, and come out at C just a little above AB, not quite half-way across. Pull through. Take a small diagonal stitch over AB to D. Start the next stitch coming out at E, over to F. The stitches are usually close together, but they also can be spaced.

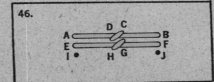

47. New England Laid—Good variation of the *Roumanian stitch* (46). It was used by pioneer women of New England to save yarns. The only difference is that the tacking down diagonal stitch CD is quite long, with C coming out near B, and D near A. The result is an interesting texture.

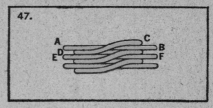

48. Bokhara Stitch—Uses the same principle. This time a long stitch AB is tacked down with small stitches CD, EF, using the same yarn.

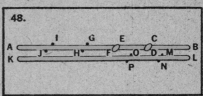

49. Spider Web Stitches—Very decorative and easy. There are several ways of working them. Try the Ribbed Spider Web: First work a number of *straight stitches* (13) from one center, pointing out, like the spokes of a wheel. You might try 6 spokes. To fill the web, bring the needle out at A between B and C. Take a step backwards and slide the needle under AB and AC. Pull through snugly. Continue taking a step backwards under AC and AD, backwards under AD and AE, and so on around as many times as necessary. Little ridges are formed on the spokes of the web. You can either fill it up or leave some of the spokes showing.

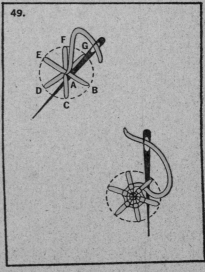

50. Couched Filling—Another form of couching. It is an easy way to fill large surfaces. A hoop or frame is essential to keep the work taut so that your pattern will be even. Yarn is laid across the shape, first vertically, then horizontally. Each intersection is tied down with a small diagonal *straight stitch* (13) or *cross stitch* (17).

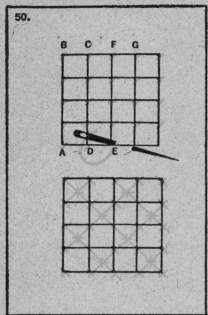

NEEDLEPOINT STITCHES

51. Half Cross Stitch—The simplest of canvas stitches. It must be worked on double-thread canvas, each row from left to right. When a row is completed, turn the work around to start again from left to right. It is good for pictures or pillows that are not subject to hard wear, and economical since there is little yarn on the back.

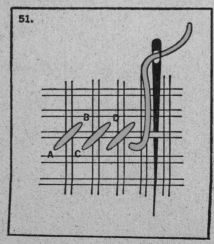

52. Continental or Tent Stitch—Considered the finest of canvas stitches, excellent for backgrounds as well as fine detail. It is good for pieces such as chairs and stools which need a hard-wearing surface. Worked from right to left on either single- or double-thread canvas. At the end of a row, turn work around and continue from right to left. A very fine *continental stitch* worked over only one thread of canvas is called Petit Point.

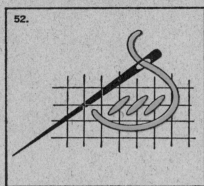

53. Basket Weave—Used mainly for backgrounds and filling shapes, can be worked on single- or double-thread canvas. It does not pull the canvas out of shape, looks smooth. It is hard wearing with a firm back which looks woven. Work on the diagonal with the needle horizontal as rows go up from right to left, then vertical as they go down from left to right.

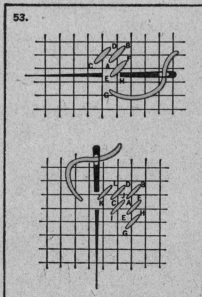

54. Straight or Upright Gobelin—Worked on single- or double-thread canvas. It is one of the oldest of canvas stitches used to imitate the woven Gobelin tapestries, giving a very effective texture. Stitches are worked vertically over 2 threads of the canvas.

If the yarn does not entirely cover the canvas, lay a strand over the row as a padding and work stitches over.

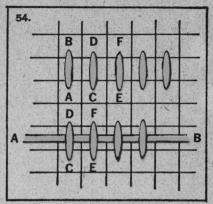

55. Encroaching Gobelin—Beautiful and effective for background and shading. It is worked over 2 horizontal rows and 1 vertical row over, slanting. Each new row starts 1 row lower and encroaches over the last canvas thread of the preceding row. The stitch can also be worked over 3, 4 or 5 horizontal rows, depending on the size of the canvas and yarn. It covers quickly.

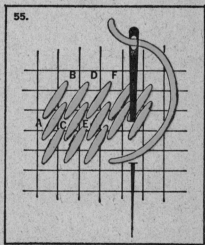

56. Bargello or Florentine Stitch—Is an *upright Gobelin* (54) usually worked in a zigzag or geometric pattern. The basic stitch is worked over 4 threads of canvas and under 2, rising and falling.   ##

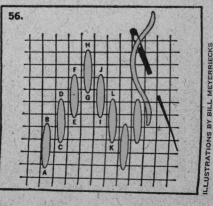

*Here are six new designs in edgings that
you can use on pillowcases, sheets, napkins and tablecloths.
You can also use them to dress up collars,
cuffs and hems on your clothing. Designs by Judith Tauber*

EASY-TO-DO CROCHET EDGINGS

MATERIALS *(for all edgings)*:
Mercerized Crochet Cotton, Size 20; steel crochet hook, No. 12, OR ANY SIZE HOOK WHICH WILL OBTAIN THE MEASUREMENT GIVEN BELOW.

Width of Edgings: A, C and D are ¾" wide; B is ⅞"; E is 1¼"; F is 1⅛". Block each edging to measurement.

Edging A *(suitable for straight or curved edges)*: Row 1: Ch 4, in 4th ch from hook make 2 dc, ch 3 and 3 dc. Ch 5; turn. Row 2: Sk first 3 dc, in next ch-3 loop make 3 dc, ch 3 and 3 dc; ch 2, sk 2 dc, dc in top of next chain. Ch 1; turn. Row 3: Sc in first dc, 2 sc in next ch-2 sp, sc in next 3 dc, sl st in ch-3 loop, ch 3, in same ch-3 loop make 2 dc, ch 3 and 3 dc. Ch 5; turn. Rpt Rows 2 and 3 for desired length, ending with last sc of Row 3. Break off and fasten.

Edging B *(suitable for straight or curved edges)*: Row 1: Ch 12, dc in 6th ch from hook, (ch 1, sk next ch, dc in next ch) twice; ch 1, sk 1 ch, 3 dc in last ch. Ch 4; turn. Row 2: 2 dc in first dc, ch 1, sk 1 dc, dc in next dc, (ch 1, dc in next dc) 3 times; 5 dc in next chain loop. Ch 1; turn. Row 3: Sc in first 6 dc, sc in next ch-1 sp, sl st in next dc, ch 4, dc in next dc, (ch 1, dc in next dc) twice; ch 1, sk next dc, 3 dc in turning ch-4 loop. Ch 4; turn. Rpt Rows 2 and 3 for desired length, ending with the sl st on Row 3. Break off and fasten.

Edging C *(suitable for straight or curved edges)*: Row 1: Ch 6; join with sl st to form ring, ch 3, in ring make 4 dc, ch 3 and 6 dc. Ch 1; turn. Row 2: Sk first dc, sc in next 5 dc, ch 3, in ch-3 loop make 4 dc, ch 3 and 4 dc; in next dc make (dc and ch 1) 4 times; sk next 3 dc, sl st in next ch-3 loop. Ch 1; turn. Row 3: (Sc in next ch-1 sp, sc in next dc) 4 times; sc in next 4 dc, ch 3, in next ch-3 loop make 4 dc, ch 3 and 4 dc; dc in next dc, sk next 3 dc, dc in top of next ch-3. Ch 1; turn. Rpt Rows 2 and 3 for desired length, ending with Row 2. Ch 1; turn. Last Row: (Sc in next ch-1 sp, sc in next dc) 4 times; sc in next 4 dc, 3 sc in next ch-3 loop, sc in next 4 dc, sc next ch-3 loop. Break off and fasten.

Edging D *(suitable for straight or curved edges)*: Row 1: Ch 11, dc in 8th ch from hook, dc in next 3 ch. Ch 5; turn. Row 2: Sk first 3 dc, dc in next dc, ch 2, dc in 3rd ch of next chain loop, 4 more dc in same chain loop. Ch 3; turn. Row 3: Sl st in first dc to form pc, sc in next 4 dc, ch 5, sk next ch-2 sp, dc in dc, 3 dc in turning ch-5 loop. Ch 5; turn. Rpt Rows 2 and 3 for desired length, ending with last sc of Row 3. Break off; fasten.

Edging E *(suitable only for straight edges)*: Row 1: Ch 13, dc in 4th ch from hook, dc in next ch, ch 2, sk 2 ch, dc in next 3 ch, ch 2, sk 2 ch, dc in last ch. Ch 5; turn. Row 2: Sk first ch-2 sp, dc in next 3 dc, ch 2, dc in next 2 dc, dc in top of turning chain. Ch 3; turn. Row 3: Sk first dc, dc in next 2 dc, 2 dc in ch-2 sp, dc in next 3 dc, 7 dc in turning chain sp, dc in top of end dc of Row 1, 5 dc along same end dc to complete scallop. Ch 1; turn. Row 4: Sc in first 5 dc, in next dc make sc, ch 4 and sc for pc; sc in next 14 dc, sc in top of turning chain. Ch 3; turn. Row 5: Sk first sc, working in back loop only of each sc, dc in next 2 sc, ch 2, sk 2 sc, dc in next 3 sc, ch 2, sk 2 sc, dc in next dc. Ch 5; turn. Row 6: Sk first ch-2 sp, dc in next 3 dc, ch 2, dc in next 2 dc, dc in top of turning chain. Ch 3; turn. Row 7: Sk first dc, dc in next 2 dc, 2 dc in ch-2 sp, dc in next 3 dc, 7 dc in turning chain sp, dc in top of end dc on next row, 5 dc along same end dc, sk next 2 free sc on previous scallop, sl st in back loop of next sc to complete scallop. Ch 1; turn. Rpt Rows 4 through 7 for desired length, ending with Row 4. Break off and fasten.

Edging F *(suitable only for straight edges)*: Row 1: Ch 12, sc in 2nd ch from hook and in each of next 10 ch. Ch 4; turn. Row 2: *Sc in first sc, ch 6, sc in last sc made, ch 4, sc in last sc made—3-pc loop made*; dc in next 10 sc. Ch 1; turn. Row 3: Sc in 10 dc, sc in top of 3-pc loop. Ch 4; turn. Row 4: Sk first 2 sc, dc in next sc, (ch 1, sk next sc, dc in next sc) 4 times. Ch 1; turn. Row 5: Sc in first dc, (sc in next ch-1 sp, sc in next dc) 4 times; 2 sc in turning ch-4 loop. Ch 4; turn. Rpt Rows 2 through 5 for desired length, ending with Row 3. Break off and fasten.

GEORGE NORDHAUSEN

Strong enough for a man, but made for a woman.

And now Secret's pretty new label makes it even more feminine.

Dry Formula Secret is a strong anti-perspirant.
But it's gentle, too, so it won't sting even
after shaving. And now it has a pretty new label
that tells you it's for a lady. Try it.

KNITTING

By LEE PARR McGRATH and JOAN RATTNER HEILMAN

KNITTING IS probably the most familiar of all the crafts. Many of us learned to knit potholders as Girl Scouts, and advanced to scarves in junior high. Some went on to even more ambitious projects, and many of us never made it past that first row.

But whether you're learning or relearning, the time to knit is certainly now. Never before have there been so many appealing colors and types of yarns, or so many fresh and imaginative patterns. And, you don't need expensive materials to achieve the most attractive creations for your home, your family or yourself.

Aside from the delight of owning something you made by hand, the very process of knitting—that quiet rhythm of clicking needles—is soothing therapy. If you want to be adventurous, try creating your own patterns and designs.

If socks bore you, knit a striking wall hanging that is pure contemporary art. Investigate the possibilities of afghans, pillows and place mats. These can enhance any style of home decorating. Follow the excitement of current fashions with romantic-looking shawls, vests or "shrink" sweaters. Once you understand the essentials of knitting, the job is easy.

As a basic guide—a refresher if you already know how to knit, a primer if you're a complete novice—here is a concise dictionary of knitting. With this to help you along, you should be able to follow any how-to instructions for a vast variety of knitted items. Clip this dictionary and keep it handy in your workbasket.

Abbreviations: Most knitting experts use the same standard symbols and abbreviations in written directions. Here's a list to help decipher any abbreviations you may have forgotten.

k	knit
p	purl
oz(s)	ounce(s)
st(s)	stitch(es)
inc(s)	increase(s)
dec(s)	decrease(s)
incl	inclusive
yo or o	yarn-over
beg	beginning
" or in	inches
tog	together
bet	between
rem	remaining
ch	chain
sc	single crochet
dc	double crochet
pat(s)	pattern(s)
lp(s)	loop(s)
sl	slip
sl st	slip stitch
MC	main color
CC	contrasting color
dp	double-pointed
psso	pass slipped stitch over last stitch worked
rnd(s)	round(s)
sk	skip
rpt	repeat
bl	block
st st	stockinette stitch
sp	space

*(asterisk): Directions immediately following * are to be repeated the specified number of times indicated, *in addition to* the first time—i.e., "repeat from * 3 times more" means 4 times in all.

( ) (parentheses): Directions should be worked as often as specified—i.e., (k 1, k 2 tog, k 3) 5 times, would mean to work what is in ( ) 5 times in all.

Argyle: Though we tend to think of Argyles as men's socks, this is only because the pattern has been so frequently used for them. Literally, Argyle is a diamond-shaped pattern (*see* FIG. 1) in two or more colors somewhat resembling the tartan of the Argyll clan (hence the name), and suitable for sweaters, scarves, mittens, vests, knee-highs and a variety of other knitting projects (*see* CHANGING COLORS).

Chart for Argyle Pattern

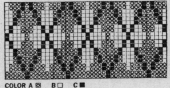

COLOR A ⊠   B ☐   C ■   Fig. 1

Binding (or Casting) Off: This makes a finished edge and locks the stitches securely in place. Knit (or purl) two stitches. Then, with the tip of the left-hand needle, lift the first of these two stitches over the second stitch and drop it off the tip of the right-hand needle (*see* FIG. 2 *on page 116*). One stitch remains on the right-hand needle and one stitch has been bound off. * Knit (or purl) the next stitch; lift the first stitch over the last stitch and off the tip of the needle. Again, one stitch remains on the right-hand needle and another stitch has been bound off. Repeat from asterisk until the required number of stitches has been bound off.

Remember that you work *two* stitches to bind off one stitch. If directions read, "k 6, bind off the next 4 sts, k 24 . . ." you must knit six stitches, then knit two *more* stitches before starting to bind off. Bind off four times. After the four stitches have been bound off, count the stitch remaining on right-hand needle as the first stitch of the next 24 stitches. When binding off, always knit the knit stitches and purl the purl stitches.

Be careful not to bind off too tightly or too loosely. The tension should be the same as the rest of the knitting.

To end off the last stitch on the bound-off edge, cut yarn leaving a six-inch end; pass the cut end through the loop of the last stitch on the right-hand needle and pull snugly (*see* FIG. 3).

Blocking: This means pinning and pressing or steaming the pieces into the proper shape. You should always block pieces before sewing them together. Place pieces, wrong side up, on a padded surface. With non-rusting pins at quarter-inch intervals, pin edges of the pieces to the padding following their correct measurements. Do not block or stretch waist or wrist ribbings. Spread a damp cloth over the knitted piece; then pass hot iron very lightly and quickly over damp cloth to create penetrating steam. Do not press the iron down or allow it to remain in one place. Allow pieces to dry before unpinning.

If you have used acrylic yarn, check the label on the skein to see if blocking is necessary. If it is, do *not* use an iron. Merely pin the pieces to the padding following their exact measurements, then dampen and allow pieces to dry before unpinning.

Buttonholes: Starting at edge, work across to where the buttonhole is to be made. Refer to BINDING-OFF directions and bind off the number of stitches specified in your instructions. Complete row. On the next row, work to the bound-off stitches, then cast on (*see* CASTING-ON *directions at right*) the same number of stitches as were bound off in previous row. Complete row.

To cast on for buttonhole: Turn work so that the needle to which the yarn is attached is held in the left hand. * Insert tip of right-hand needle into first stitch on left-hand needle and knit one stitch, leaving the original stitch on the left-hand needle. With tip of left-hand needle, slip the new stitch from the right to the left-hand needle. You have

Binding (or Casting) Off

Fig. 2

Fig. 3

Buttonholes

Fig. 4

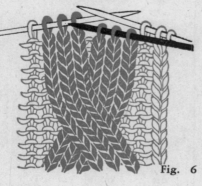

Fig. 5

Cable Stitch

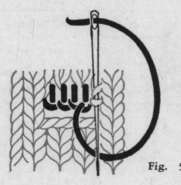

Fig. 6

Casting On

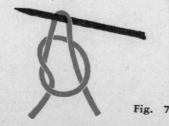

Fig. 7

now cast on, or added, one stitch. Repeat from * until the specified number of stitches have been cast on (*see* FIG. 4), then turn work again and continue to follow instructions.

When the garment has been completed, work buttonhole stitch around each buttonhole, using matching yarn and being careful not to work tightly (*see* FIG. 5).

Cable Stitch (*Simple*): This is done by crossing or twisting various sets of stitches at given intervals while knitting. Slip the number of stitches specified in directions onto a cable-stitch holder or onto a double-pointed needle (*see* FIG. 6). Hold these stitches in front or in back of the work, according to your instructions. Now work the same number of stitches from left-hand needle onto right-hand needle. Then work the stitches from the cable holder. You have produced a simple cable. Continue working as your instructions indicate. Cables may have two or more divisions of stitches. However, the cabling operation always remains the same as for the simple cable stitch.

Cable-stitch Holders: These come in different sizes and shapes to accommodate different yarns and hold the stitches out of your way until needed. Substitute a double-pointed knitting needle, or even a toothpick.

Casting On: This operation puts the first row of stitches on the needle. Measure off about a yard or two of yarn (or about an inch for each stitch you are going to cast on). Make a slip knot at this point by making a loop of yarn; then pull another small loop through it (*see* FIG. 7). Place the slip knot on one needle and pull one end to tighten. Hold needle in right hand. Hold both strands of yarn in the palm of your left hand securely but not rigidly. Slide your left thumb and forefinger between the two strands and spread these two fingers out so that you have formed a triangle of yarn (*see* FIG. 8). Your thumb should hold the free end of yarn, your forefinger the yarn from the ball, and the needle the first stitch. You are now in position to cast on. * Bring the needle in your right hand toward you, slip the tip of the needle under the front strand of loop on left thumb (*see* FIG. 9). Then, with the needle, catch the strand of yarn that is on your left forefinger (*see* FIG. 10), draw it through the thumb loop to form a stitch on needle (*see* FIG. 11). Holding the stitch on the needle with the right index finger, slip loop off left thumb (*see* FIG. 12). Tighten up the stitch on needle by pulling the freed strand back with left thumb, thus bringing yarn back in position for casting on more

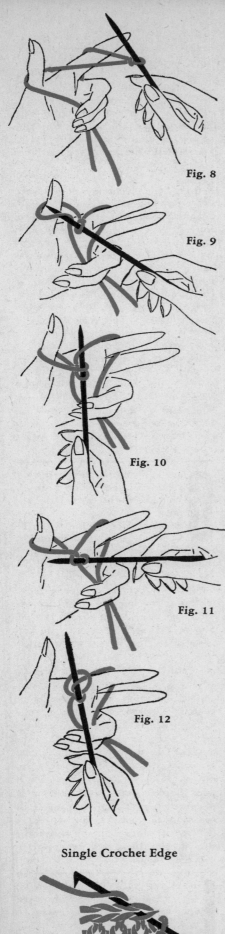

Fig. 8

Fig. 9

Fig. 10

Fig. 11

Fig. 12

Single Crochet Edge

Fig. 13

(*back to* FIG. 8). Do not cast on too tightly. Repeat from * until you have the number of stitches specified in your instructions.

Changing Colors: Always join in a new color on a knit row. Start knitting with the new color at the indicated stitch, leaving a few inches of yarn to be woven in later on wrong side. Or, you can join the two colors together with a loose knot, leaving a few inches of each color. When you have finished the work, pull the knot through to the wrong side; untie the knot and weave in the ends (*see* JOINING YARN).

If you are changing colors constantly, as in Argyles or Fair Isles, don't break the yarn each time; use bobbins or carry it across the wrong side loosely to maintain gauge. When working with two or more colors, lock strands by picking up the new color from *under* the dropped color, or twist new color around previous color to prevent making holes.

Crocheted Edge: Crocheting is often used to finish the edges of knitted work. It can be done with a single crochet stitch which makes a stand-up edge, or with a slip stitch which makes a flat edge.

Working from right to left unless otherwise specified, work stitches evenly along edge, making two or three stitches in the same place at the corners to keep the work flat. Do not work too tightly or the edges will curl.

Single Crochet (sc): Make a loop of yarn on the crochet hook. Insert hook through knitted edge. Catch yarn (*see* FIG. 13) and draw through (*see* FIG. 14). Pass the yarn over the hook (*see* FIG. 15) and draw it through both loops on hook (*see* FIG. 16).

Slip Stitch (sl st): Make a loop of yarn on the crochet hook. Insert hook through knitted edge, catch the yarn (*see* FIG. 17) and, with one motion, draw it through both the knitted edge and the loop on hook (*see* FIG. 18).

Crochet Hook: For picking up dropped stitches or adding a crocheted edge. The size required is usually specified in the knitting directions.

Decreasing (*dec*): This means reducing the number of stitches in a given area to shape your work. This applies when shaping a skirt, a yoke on a garment, or to shape front, neck and armhole edges. Two different methods for decreasing are as follows:

1. Knit (*see* FIG. 19) or purl (*see* FIG. 20) two stitches together by inserting right-hand needle through the loops of two stitches on left-hand needle at the same time; then complete the stitch. If you work through the *front* loops of the stitches in the usual way, your

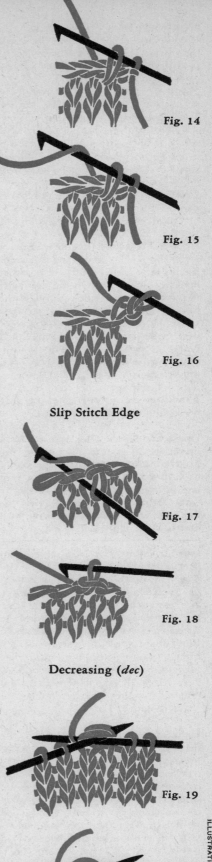

Fig. 14

Fig. 15

Fig. 16

Slip Stitch Edge

Fig. 17

Fig. 18

Decreasing (*dec*)

Fig. 19

Fig. 20

decreasing stitch will slant to the right. If you work through the *back* loops of the stitches, your decreasing stitch will slant to the left. This is written k 2 tog (p 2 tog).

2. Insert right-hand needle through the stitch on the left-hand needle, but instead of working it, just slip it off onto the right-hand needle. Work the next stitch in the usual way. With the tip of the left-hand needle, lift the slipped stitch over the last stitch worked and off the tip of the right-hand needle (*see* FIG. 21). Your decreasing stitch will slant to the left. This is written as sl 1, k 1, psso.

Dropped Stitches: If you have let a stitch slip off the needle and it has unraveled or run down a bit, use a crochet hook to pick it up. On the knit side, insert the crochet hook through the loop, front to back, of the dropped stitch. Hook the horizontal strand of yarn in the row above (*see* FIG. 22) and pull it through the loop on hook. Continue in this way until loop on hook reaches knitting needle. Put loop on needle, being careful not to twist it. Do this in reverse on purl side, inserting hook through *back* (*see* FIG. 23).

Duplicate Stitch: This is used for a decorative effect, after the knitting has been completed. With another color yarn threaded into a tapestry or yarn needle, duplicate the knitted stitches by embroidering over them, so that the duplicate stitches look the same as a knitted-in design. (*see* FIG. 24).

Fair Isle: Often called Norwegian or Scandinavian knitting. The term describes working a pattern while knitting, using two or more colors simultaneously on the same row (unused color carried loosely across on the wrong side until needed). Fair Isle patterns are usually worked from a chart which indicates, by symbol and legend, where each color is to be used. Small geometric patterns are typical, and this style is popular for sweaters, gloves and socks.

Fisherman or Aran Knits: Originally these garments were knitted in traditional patterns with naturally moisture-repellent, cream-colored wool. Today, pattern instructions covering authentic stitches are available and you may choose either the natural, unbleached wool yarn to reproduce the original effect, or choose knitting worsted in colors. You can buy the imported, slightly oily, unprocessed wool actually used by the fishermen. Because it has water-repelling properties it is recommended for ski sweaters.

Four-needle Knitting: Loosely cast on required number of stitches, dividing them equally among three double-

Fig. 21

Dropped Stitches

Fig. 22

Fig. 23

Duplicate Stitch

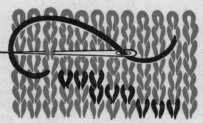

Fig. 24

Four-needle Knitting

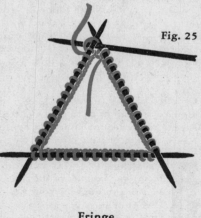

Fig. 25

Fringe

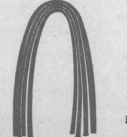

Fig. 26

pointed needles. Being careful not to twist stitches, make a triangle of the three needles, holding in left hand, with the first cast-on stitch held close to the last (*see* FIG. 25). Use the fourth needle to knit the stitches from the first needle in the regular way, then with free needle knit the stitches from the second needle; with next free needle knit next stitches from third needle to complete round.

Fringe: Even a beginner's project, such as a scarf, will take on a finished, professional look with the addition of fringe.

To make fringe: Decide how long you want the fringe to be. Cut a cardboard square ½" larger than desired fringe length. Wind yarn 50 times around cardboard (enough to make 10 or more fringes). Then cut strands at one edge, making strands more than double the desired fringe length. Hold two (or more) strands together, fold them in half to form a loop (*see* FIG. 26). Insert crochet hook through the edge of the knitting from back to front and draw loop through (*see* FIG. 27); then draw ends through loop and tighten (*see* FIGS. 28–29). Repeat this process at even intervals along the edges where fringe is wanted.

Garter Stitch: This effect is achieved when every row is knitted. Both sides look the same; every two rows of knitting forms a ridge (*see* FIG. 30). To work the garter stitch on double-pointed or circular needles, knit 1 round, then purl 1 round.

Gauge: Instructions include a gauge indicating the number of stitches and rows, or rounds, to the inch. *It is important to match this gauge.* If you knit fewer stitches per inch than the gauge, your work will be too big; if you knit more stitches per inch work will be too small. Using the recommended yarn and needles, knit a small square sample swatch. Block swatch and then measure it. Count stitches and rows to see how many stitches or rows you have to the inch (*see* FIG. 31). If your sample shows more stitches (or rows) to the inch than the gauge calls for, try larger needles. If your sample contains fewer stitches (or rows) to the inch than the gauge calls for, try smaller needles. In all cases, use the recommended yarn and the proper size needles to achieve the recommended gauge.

Increasing (*inc*): This means adding stitches in a given area to shape your work. There are three ways to increase as follows:

1. *To increase by knitting twice into the same stitch:* Knit the stitch in the usual way thr...

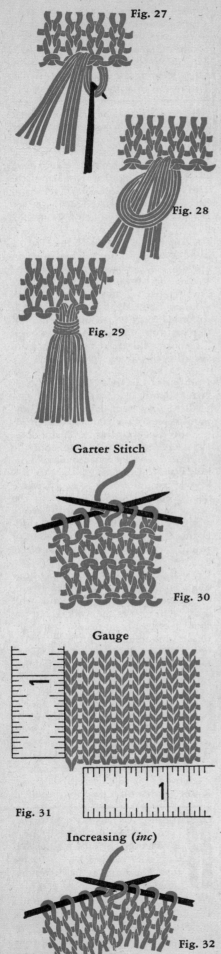

Fig. 27

Fig. 28

Fig. 29

Garter Stitch

Fig. 30

Gauge

Fig. 31

Increasing (*inc*)

Fig. 32

FIG. 32), but, before dropping it from the left-hand needle, knit another stitch on the same loop by placing the needle into the *back* of the stitch (*see* FIG. 33). Slip the original stitch off your left-hand needle. You have made two stitches from one stitch.

2. *To increase by knitting between the stitches:* Insert the tip of the right-hand needle under the strand of yarn *between* the stitch you've just worked and the following stitch and slip it onto the tip of the left-hand needle (*see* FIG. 34). Now work into the back of this new loop (*see* FIG. 35).

3. *To increase by "yarn-over":* Pass the yarn over the right-hand needle to create another stitch (*see* FIG. 36). On the next row, work this yarn-over (yo) as a stitch.

Instant Knits: These are knits done on jumbo needles (up to an inch in diameter), using three to six strands of yarn at once. The combination of jumbo needles and multiple strands of yarn creates huge stitches; therefore work is very fast. *Caution:* Garments may sag if knitted too loosely.

Joining Yarn: When you come to the end of a ball of yarn, it is best to join a new ball at the edge of the work. End a row with the old yarn and start the next row with the new yarn.

If you must join the yarn in the middle of a row, tie the new yarn to the old with a loose knot, leaving a few inches of each end. When you have finished the work, pull knot through to wrong side. Untie knot; weave ends in.

To work in a loose end, thread it into a blunt needle. Now pass the needle through the stitches on the wrong side, or through the edge stitches, being sure you go through enough stitches so that the loose end will stay securely in place.

Knit (*k*): Hold the needle with the cast-on stitches in your left hand (*see* FIG. 37). Pick up the other needle in your right hand. With yarn from ball in back of work, insert the tip of right-hand needle from left to right through the front loop of the first stitch on the left-hand needle (*see* FIG. 38). Holding both needles in this position with left hand, wrap the yarn over your little finger, under your two middle fingers and over the forefinger of your right hand. Hold the yarn firmly, but loosely enough so that it will slide through your fingers as you knit. Return right-hand needle to right hand.

With right forefinger, pass the yarn under (from right to left) and then over (from left to right) the tip of the right-hand needle, forming a loop on needle (*see* FIG. 39). Now draw this loop through the stitch on the left-hand

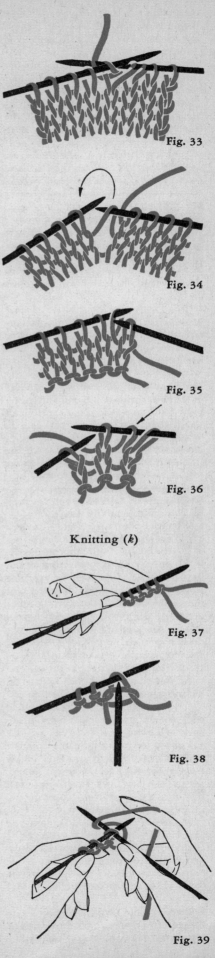

Fig. 33

Fig. 34

Fig. 35

Fig. 36

Knitting (*k*)

Fig. 37

Fig. 38

Fig. 39

needle (see FIG. 40). Slip the original stitch off the left-hand needle, leaving the new stitch on the right-hand needle (see FIG. 41).

Keep stitches loose enough so that you can slide them along the needles, but firm enough so they do not slide when you don't want them to. Continue until you have knitted all the stitches from the left-hand needle onto the right-hand needle.

To start the next row, pass the needle with the stitches on it to the left hand so that it becomes the left-hand needle.

Markers: Small metal or plastic rings that you slip on your needle to mark a specific place. They help you keep track of the number of stitches in intricate patterns. Use also to mark where increases or decreases occur.

Measuring: Lay the work on a flat surface to measure. Do not include the cast-on edge, but start with the first row when measuring.

Multiple: Multiple means the number of stitches required for one pattern repeat. So, if the pattern is a multiple of six stitches, the number of stitches to be cast on should be divisible by six. If directions call for a multiple of six stitches plus two, two extra stitches are required at end of cast-on row.

Needles: Choose your knitting needles carefully. Look for lightness, flexibility and smooth points (neither too sharp nor too blunt). Aluminum or plastic needles are the two most popular. Steel needles are used for very fine work (their sizes are just the reverse of the regular needles: The larger the number, the finer the needle). Since your manner of knitting governs the size needle you need, a beginner would be wise to have three sizes of needles on hand: The one called for in the instructions, one size larger if you knit tightly, one size smaller if you knit loosely. *Straight needles* have single pointed ends and are used in pairs for knitting back and forth in rows. They are 10", 12" or 14" long, as a rule, and come in sizes from 0 through 15. The smaller the number, the finer the needle. Jumbo needles (see INSTANT KNITS), popular for super-speedy knitting, come in sizes up to one inch in diameter.

A circular needle is used for knitting in rounds wherever seams are to be avoided, as in skirts, sleeves, turtlenecks and so forth. The stitches are knitted continuously from one tip to the other in a complete circle (see FIG. 42).

Double-pointed needles (dp needles) are straight needles with points at each end. They come in sets of four or five

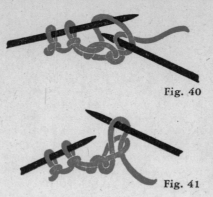

Fig. 40

Fig. 41

Circular Needle

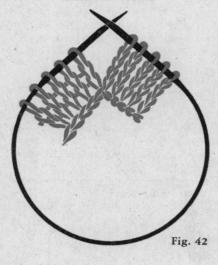

Fig. 42

Picking Up Along the Edge
(pick up and knit)

Fig. 43

Purling (p)

Fig. 44

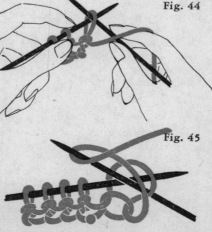

Fig. 45

needles. Stitches can be divided onto three or four needles according to instructions (see FOUR-NEEDLE KNITTING); the spare needle is used to work over the stitches on the next needle which then becomes the spare needle. This results in a small tubular piece.

Pass Slipped Stitch Over (psso): This is a decrease stitch. After slipping one stitch from the left-hand needle to the right-hand needle, and being careful to keep it in position, work next stitch. Then—with the tip of the left-hand needle—lift the slipped stitch over the last stitch and off the tip of the needle.

Picking Up Along the Edge (pick up and knit): To pick up stitches along an armhole or neck edge, hold the right side of the work toward you. * Insert knitting needle into the edge, wrap yarn around needle and pull it through to form a stitch on needle (see FIG. 43). Repeat from * until you have enough picked-up stitches, being sure they are spaced evenly along the edge.

Pompons: Cut two circles of cardboard slightly larger than the diameter of the desired pompon. Cut a ½" hole in the center of each circle. Hold circles together and wrap yarn over the outer edge and through the hole until the cardboard is covered all around and the hole is filled. Cut through the yarn following the cardboard edges. Separate the two circles just enough to tie the center of yarn strands with a strong string; knot securely. Remove cardboard and trim evenly. Use ends of string to attach the pompons in place.

Purl (p): Purling is the reverse of knitting. To purl, hold the needle with the stitches in your left hand with the yarn in *front* of the work. Insert the tip of the right-hand needle from right to left through the front loop of the first stitch on the left-hand needle (see FIG. 44). With your right hand holding the yarn in the same manner as to knit, but in *front* of the needles, pass the yarn over the tip of the right-hand needle, then under it, forming a loop on needle (see FIG. 45). Holding the yarn firmly, so that it won't slip off, draw this loop through the stitch on left-hand needle (see FIG. 46). Slip the original stitch off the left-hand needle (see FIG. 47), leaving new stitch on right-hand needle.

Ribbing: Usually worked on an even number of stitches, ribbing is achieved by alternating knit and purl stitches on the same row. The result is an elastic texture. After working the first row, the knit stitches facing you should be knitted; the purl stitches should be purled. The yarn should be in back of your work for knitti'

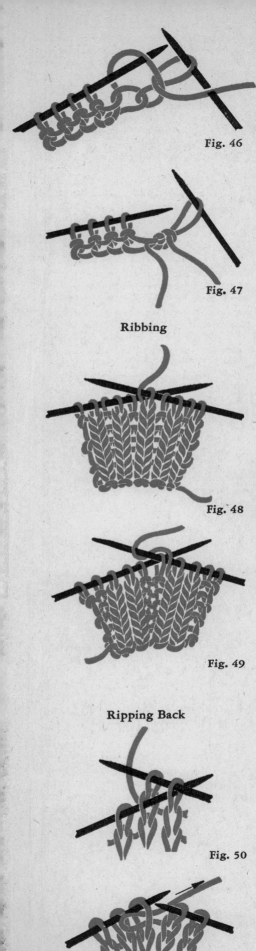

Fig. 46

Fig. 47

Ribbing

Fig. 48

Fig. 49

Ripping Back

Fig. 50

Fig. 51

work for purling. The pattern for ribbing is governed by the number of knit stitches and purl stitches employed for each rib. FIG. 48 shows k 1, p 1 ribbing. FIG. 49 shows k 2, p 2 ribbing.

Ripping Back: If a mistake has been made and you have to rip back only a few stitches or rip back only a row or two, it is best to do it stitch by stitch by *un*-knitting the stitches. Insert the left-hand needle into the stitch of the row *below* the stitch you want to rip while that stitch is still on the right-hand needle (*see* FIG. 50). Drop the top stitch from the right-hand needle, leaving the stitch below it on left-hand needle (*see* FIG. 51). Pull yarn through dropped stitch. Continue as necessary.

Ripping Back Whole Rows: If you must rip back a lot of knitting, take the work off the needles and rip to within one row past the mistake. Carefully replace the stitches as follows: Hold the work in your left hand with the yarn end at the left. Starting at the right, using a smaller size needle, insert the needle from the back to the front of each stitch across until you have all of the stitches back on the needle (*see* FIG. 52). Change to original needle and continue.

Seaming: After blocking you are ready to seam. Thread matching yarn into a tapestry or yarn needle and join as follows:

To backstitch seams: Being careful to match rows, edges and patterns, pin the pieces together, right sides facing. Sew edges together with running stitches and a back stitch every inch for strength—*do not sew too tightly or the work will pucker, or too loosely so that there will be holes* (*see* FIG. 53).

To weave seams: Place pieces side by side, right side up, patterns matching and edges together. From right side of fabric take a small running stitch along seam edge of one piece, * then take a stitch along seam edge of matching piece; take a small stitch along edge of first piece. Repeat from * until the entire seam is joined without puckering or leaving holes (*see* FIG. 54).

To thread a tapestry needle with yarn: Fold the yarn over shaft of the needle and pull it tightly to form a sharp crease. Slip it off the needle; thread needle with creased yarn.

Seed or Moss Stitch: Usually worked on an uneven number of stitches per row. Knit and purl stitches are alternated to produce a work that is the same on both sides. If Row 1 calls for k 1, p 1, k 1 etc. across entire row, ending with k 1, instructions for Row 2 will be the same so that, when a knit stitch faces you, you purl it; and when a purl stitch faces you, you knit it (*see* FIG. 55).

Slip Stitch (*sl st*): Insert the tip of the

Ripping Back Whole Rows

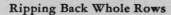
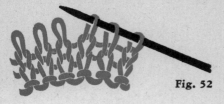

Fig. 52

Seaming

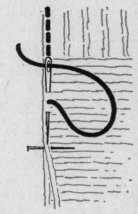

Fig. 53

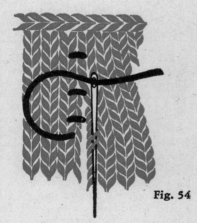

Fig. 54

Seed or Moss Stitch

Fig. 55

Slip Stitch (*sl st*)

Fig. 56

right-hand needle into the next stitch on left-hand needle, as if to purl, unless otherwise directed. Slip this stitch off the left-hand needle onto the right, without working it (see FIG. 56).

Stockinette Stitch (*st st*): When you alternate one knit row and one purl row the result is a stockinette stitch. Each side is different. The knit side is the smooth side (see FIG. 57). The purl side is the nubby side (see FIG. 58). If the purl side is used for the right side, it is called "reverse stockinette stitch." When working the stockinette stitch on a circular needle, knit every round.

Tassel: Cut a piece of cardboard slightly longer than the length you want your finished tassel to be. Wrap yarn around cardboard until you have the desired fullness (or according to your instructions). Tie a double strand of yarn securely through all strands at edge of cardboard at top; leave the ends long (see FIG. 59). Clip through strands at opposite edge, removing cardboard. To finish, wrap another piece of yarn around strands, about ½ inch down from top, and tie (see FIG. 60). Using a tapestry or yarn needle, sew tassel to edge of finished item.

Winding Yarn: Most yarn is already wound in balls or in "pull-out" *skeins*, ready to use. To wind from a *hank* of yarn, have another person loop the hank over his hands, stretching it out quite tautly. Wind the yarn loosely around four fingers about 20 times; slip this ball off fingers but hold in hand; then, to prevent stretching, wind yarn around the ball *and* your fingers about 20 times; slip off fingers. Turn ball and continue winding as before, changing direction occasionally to keep the ball round (see FIG. 61).

Work Even: Work without increasing or decreasing.

Yarn-over (*yo or o*): Pass the yarn over the right-hand needle after finishing one stitch and before starting the next stitch to create another stitch. *If you are knitting*, bring the yarn under the needle to the front, then over the needle to the back. *If you are purling*, wind the yarn around the needle once. On the next row, work all yarn-overs as stitches (see FIG. 62).

Yarns: Knitting instructions specify the type of yarn to be used. Unless you are an experienced knitter, it is unwise to substitute a yarn other than that recommended. The wrapper on each skein of yarn carries the information you need, and tells you if the yarn is mothproof, colorfast and pre-shrunk.

Stockinette Stitch (*st st*)

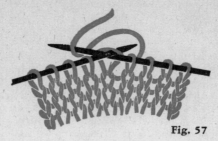

Fig. 57

Fig. 58

Tassel

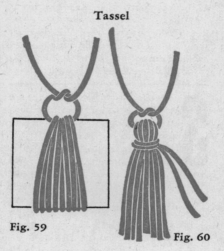

Fig. 59

Fig. 60

Winding Yarn

Fig. 61

Yarn-over (*yo or o*)

Fig. 62

Be sure to buy enough yarn to finish your project. Dye lots vary and if you have to purchase additional yarn, there may be a slight but noticeable color variation.

Yarns differ in fiber, twist, weight and texture. The number of strands twisted together are described by ply: 2-, 3- or 4-ply. The size of the ply determines how heavy the yarn is.

Fibers
Wool: A natural fiber, wool is the traditional favorite, available everywhere in a wide range of colors. The elasticity of wool is a great plus. Try, if possible, to buy wool that is pre-shrunk, mothproof and colorfast.
Orlon, acrylics and other man-made synthetics: These duplicate almost any texture of wool yarn and have their own virtues, since they are machine washable and non-allergenic. Blends are usually made of synthetics and wool.
Cotton: This yarn/thread varies in size from tatting cotton (the thinnest thread) to rug yarn (the thickest). Some threads are mercerized to give luster. Knitting with cotton presents problems, because work tends to slant.
Mohairs and angoras: These fluffy yarns (goat or rabbit hair) can be knitted for beautiful results. However, beginners should be warned—these yarns do not rip out as easily as other yarns, and, because of their fuzzy texture, it isn't always easy to see what's happening.

Yarn Types
Knitting worsted: A hard-wearing, reasonably priced, 4-ply yarn suggested for a beginner.
Sport yarn: A finer and firmer yarn than knitting worsted, having a twist that makes it wear well. Suitable for all kinds of sportswear and men's socks.
Baby and fingering yarns: Softer yarns adaptable for finer results and especially suitable for infants' garments. Be sure to check for shrink resistance.
Rug yarn: Extra-bulky yarn used for potholders, pillows, rugs and other items that can be attractively made with large stitches. Avoid rug yarn that has too much stretch. ∎

Knitting Needs and Aids

1. *Straight needles*
2. *Circular needle*
3. *dp needles*
4. *Needle guards*
5. *Stitch holder*
6. *Cable-stitch holder*
7. *Yarn bobbins*
8. *Needle gauge*
9. *Stitch counter*
10. *Markers*
11. *Crochet hooks*
12. *Steel measuring tape*
13. *Yarn needles*

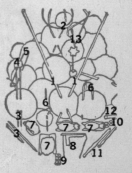